The Magic of Serpents

The Magic of Serpents

Scott Irvine

MOON
BOOKS
Winchester, UK
Washington, USA

JOHN HUNT PUBLISHING

First published by Moon Books, 2023
Moon Books is an imprint of John Hunt Publishing Ltd., No. 3 East Street, Alresford
Hampshire SO24 9EE, UK
office@jhpbooks.net
www.johnhuntpublishing.com
www.moon-books.net

For distributor details and how to order please visit the 'Ordering' section on our website.

Text copyright: Scott Irvine 2022

ISBN: 978 1 80341 056 2
978 1 80341 057 9 (ebook)
Library of Congress Control Number: 2021950037

A CIP catalogue record for this book is available from the British Library.

Design: Matthew Greenfield

UK: Printed and bound by CPI Group (UK) Ltd, Croydon, CR0 4YY
Printed in North America by CPI GPS partners

We operate a distinctive and ethical publishing philosophy in
all areas of our business, from our global network of authors to
production and worldwide distribution.

Contents

Preface

The Fall of Man

Genesis 3, 1-20 Good News Bible (1976)

1   The serpent was more devious than any beast of the field that the Lord God had made.

2   And the woman said to the serpent, 'We can eat the fruit of the trees in the garden'.

3   'But the fruit of the tree which is at the centre of the garden, God has said we shall not eat it, nor shall we even touch it, or we will die'.

4   And the serpent said to the woman, 'You will surely not die'.

5   'For God does know that on the day you eat the fruit from the tree at the centre of the garden, your eyes will be opened and you shall be like the gods in knowing good and evil'.

6   And when the woman saw that the tree was good for food and that it was pleasant to the eye, a tree that could make her wise, so she took the fruit and ate it. She then gave the fruit for her husband to eat.

7   And the eyes of them both were opened and they saw that

they were naked so made themselves clothes from fig leaves sewn together.

8   And they heard the voice of the Lord while walking in the garden in the cool of the day causing them to hide from his presence amongst the trees in the garden.

9   And the Lord called to Adam.

10   And Adam replied, 'I heard your voice and I was afraid so hid myself because I was naked'.

11   And the Lord asked 'Who told you that you were naked? Have you eaten from the tree I commanded you not to eat?'

12   And the man replied 'It was the woman who gave me the fruit from the tree, and I ate it'.

13   And the Lord said to the woman 'What have you done?' And the woman replied 'The serpent tempted me, and I ate it'.

14   And the Lord said to the serpent 'Because of what you have done, you are cursed above all cattle and every beast in the field. On your belly shall you live and dust is what you shall eat for all the days of your life'.

15   'And I will put an animosity between you and the woman and between your seed and her seed. It shall bruise your head and heel'.

16   And to the woman He said 'I will greatly increase your sorrow and you will suffer much pain giving birth. Your desire shall be to your husband and he shall rule over you'.

17   And He said to Adam 'Because you listened to your wife and ate from the tree that I commanded you not to, you are cursed to live off the land and eat from it for all of the days of your life'.

18   'Thorns and thistles will prick you and you shall eat the grain of the field'.

19   'In the sweat of your face, you shall eat bread until you return to the ground, for out of it you were taken for you are dust, and into dust you shall return'.

20   Adam called his wife Eve because she was the mother of all.

These twenty verses from the beginning of the Bible have demonised the serpent and cursed all women to be ruled by men for over 2,000 years. The story of the serpent in the Garden of Eden is probably the most well-known about a snake ever told. You cannot mention Adam and Eve without the serpent tempting humanity with the knowledge of good and evil. However, as ancient the story in the Old Testament is, the symbolism of the snake is many thousands of years older. Stories of the serpent can be found in all ancient myths across the planet and is one of the most powerful and recognised symbols in the human consciousness. It represents the creative force within nature, the transformation from one age to another, shedding the old to grow new worlds and evolve into the future.

So, is the serpent a force for the good or an evil demon? As we all know, it is the victors that write the history, those in power that accuse their enemy as the devious untrusted serpent, the evil abomination cursed by God. The Mother Goddess of the Sumerians, Tiamat, the Mother of Life, had guided our hunter-gatherer ancestors through the Stone Age, but with the rise of the Babylonian gods, she became a threat to their control over humanity and in their eyes became a demonic 'She Dragon', of chaos with an army of serpents at her disposal. Only when she was defeated, the Babylonian priests were able to put women in a lesser role than men in every circumstance.

I believe the serpent has been given a bad press because it represents universal knowledge and truth, something the powers in control of populations have been trying to supress for millennia for fear of losing their dominance over their subjects, congregations and populations. The serpent promotes learning so the spirit within can develop and grow, shedding off its skin, representing the eternal soul, shedding its body to allow rebirth to occur in a new existence.

Throughout this book, I will be exploring the serpent from its first mention in the Sumerian cuneiform clay tablets written over 5,000 years ago in what is now Iraq, through hiss-story to how the ancient reptile is perceived today. Over the past few millennia, the serpent has been associated with dark demonic overtones because it represents knowledge and truth, something the Eagles (the church and government) and the Lions (the crown and major corporations) have spent a good deal of their time supressing.

To be honest, snakes terrify me. One of my earliest memories of a serpent was the female rock python, Kaa, in Disney's *Jungle Book*. Her hypnotic eyes and voice stirred a deep sense of distrust towards the slithering, scaly reptile. As a kid, we used to hunt for adders on the waste ground behind our estate and prod them with sticks until they slithered away into the undergrowth. We feared their poisonous fangs, that we were warned about by our parents, would deliver a lingering and painful death. I quickly grew out of that and thought no more of snakes until the rock star Alice Cooper announced 'Schools Out', with a boa constrictor wrapped around his neck in the early 70's. Snakes became cool.

For our thirtieth birthdays, a group of us celebrated with a three-week holiday touring Morocco. In Marrakesh, we were fascinated by the snake charmers who tempted us to have a cobra placed around our neck. Andrew was the only one brave or stupid enough to agree. When he asked for the snake to be removed, the snake charmer only smiled and shrugged his shoulders. How we laughed. Then the charmer began poking the snake, agitating it enough to expand its neck and hiss loudly. Andrew, beginning to panic insisted the snake was removed at once but the charmer insisted he would only remove the snake if we all paid him to do so. Reluctantly we all paid up when we realised it was the only way we could rescue our friend, once we had finished taking photos of course. We learnt a good lesson that day. Snakes are not for wearing unless you are Shiva or Alice Cooper.

On a simple level, the snake represents the shedding, or letting go of outdated thoughts and habits. On a religious level, the serpent is an evil abomination cursed by God and never to be trusted. On a spiritual level, the serpent is a feminine earthly power that uncoils up through the chakras to unite with her masculine heavenly love. On a philosophical level, the serpent represents the human ego that comes between the higher and lower selves of the mind.

The serpent is an interesting character on all levels, some for a force for good, others a power of evil, but on most levels, the nature of the snake is somewhere between the two.

The Magic of Serpents

In almost every ancient culture across the world, the serpent has been regarded as one of the major creation deities. Their spirit is the vibrational energy from which everything that exists is created. It is no coincidence that frequency waves resemble a moving serpent. Our early ancestors knew the power of the creative snake, but how could they without 'outside' help? Did Aliens reveal it to them? Interdimensional beings? An unknown advanced civilization like the Atlanteans? Is it possible they learnt it by connecting to the Earth spirits that pervade all of nature? One thing for sure from the evidence of early myths from around the world, the power of the snake is the creative force of the universe, the energy that generates all life on our planet. The energy of the serpent is transformation, regeneration and rebirth. It is ancient, it is wisdom and it is the order from the chaos of darkness.

With a good understanding of the ancient nature of the serpent, we can look at what it means to have a serpent as a spiritual guide. First, we must remember that of all the creatures that exist on our planet, humanity was the last to be created. We had to learn from our animal friends how to survive and become the species we are today. The animals understood the purpose of existence on Earth because they have lived it for millions of years. We learnt from them what we could and could not eat, the importance of communicating with each other and how to develop family structures. It is through our collaborating with each other that we learnt language that developed into ceremonies and rituals allowing us to talk with the Earth, the animal spirits and the gods. Through these ceremonies, we learnt that each animal possessed its own unique spiritual being and power that could be bestowed upon us so we could help ourselves and others. With the help of animal guides, humanity could attain the balance between their physical and the spiritual selves. The shaman, witchdoctor and medicine men and women of ancient cultures would dress up in the skins of the animal they wished to communicate with, induced into a trance through drugs, drumming, dance and chanting either alone or with the rest of the tribe.

When you call on the power of an animal, you are asking to be drawn into complete harmony with the strength of that creature's nature. Your spiritual animal becomes your teacher allowing you to grow and connect with Mother Earth. Learn to respect and honour every living thing as a teacher, see the spirit in everything and Mother Earth will begin to reveal her secrets. The snake evokes strong feelings of both fascination and fear; fascination because of its sleek wavy body that glides across the ground and through the water with ease. Fear because of its vicious bite, poisonous or not, and the speed it can move across the ground can surprise some people. They are not slow.

Out of more than 3,000 species of snakes in the world, around 600 are venomous and over 200 are considered medically important. Medicinal uses of snake venom include its anti-coagulant properties to treat strokes, heart attacks and pulmonary embolisms. It can reduce high blood pressure and treat thrombosis, arthritis and some cancers. Snake venom is most commonly used as a muscle relaxant to reduce spasms and back and neck pain, fibromyalgia, multiple sclerosis and seizure disorders. Snakes are found in all corners of the planet except Antarctica, Greenland, Iceland and New Zealand.

The spirit of the snake as a universal creative force can bring the beauty of nature and the connection to Mother Earth to life again for you. The power of the snake spirit is the magic of creation as it embodies sexuality, psychic energy, alchemy, fertility and promotes ascension into the higher realms. It is the energy of wholeness, cosmic consciousness and promotes the ability to experience anything without fear. It is the knowledge that all things are equal in creation. The serpent represents complete understanding and acceptance of the opposing male and female forces within each organism, creating a union of two into one, producing raw divine energy.

On a personal level, the serpent teaches that you are a universal being. By accepting all aspects of your life at any given moment, you can bring about transformation of the creative fire from within. This fire energy, when working on the material plane creates passion and desire, procreation and physical vitality. On the emotional plane, it becomes drive and ambition, creation and resolution. On the mental plane, the fire becomes intellect and charisma, power and leadership. When the snake energy reaches the spiritual plane, it becomes wisdom and understanding, wholeness (holiness) and complete connection to the spirit of the entire universe.

When your life feels unproductive, become the snake energy; release the old skin of your present situation to bring about a new reality where the rhythm of the snake dances in tune with the heartbeat of Mother Earth delivering you through the darkness into a new consciousness.

Be like a river, slowly winding its way towards the sea knowing that each atom of water represents you being accepted by the whole of creation. Be like a snake and create new worlds through writing, poetry, song, painting or sculpture, or changing your perception of your personal world by changing the way you look at the world. Think and be more positive and the universe will collaborate to bring you positive outcomes. Become a positive force in your world. What you think, you become, what you feel, you attract and what you imagine, you create.

A serpent does not go out of its way to be hostile, unless hunting for food. It will protect its family vehemently, and if cornered will fight to the death to escape. If a serpent can, it will remove itself from confrontation, it does not need to prove itself and neither should you. Do not be like a bull to a red rag and easily triggered. Be the bigger person, turn the other cheek and walk away.

Learn from the serpent and become a better person that is at one with themselves, Mother Earth and the universe.

The Babylonian Snake Lord

It is probably best to acknowledge that the serpent is much, much older than even the first human to wander the Earth. The serpent is ancient, older than the hills, literally, the species witnessed the rise of the Rocky Mountains and the Indian continent drive into mainland Asia to produce the still growing Himalaya Mountains. They saw too, Australia break away from Antarctica and the Polar Regions free from continental ice sheets.

The first snakes slithered across a world that was ruled by plant eating dinosaurs like the stegosaurus, the triceratops and the torosaurus. The world belonged to the reptiles and the prince of the reptiles was the serpent. With an ample supply of dinosaur eggs and small mammals at hand, the serpent never went hungry. Global temperatures rose constantly throughout the last stages of the Jurassic period with more and more volcanic eruptions spewing out massive amounts of carbon gases into the atmosphere trapping the heat of the sun within Earth's stratosphere. Then, the volcanoes must have stopped because at the beginning of the Cretaceous Period 140 million years ago, the planet began to cool to a moderate average temperature of 35°C. Many of the plant eating giant lizards died out along with many large marine reptiles leaving the way for the Earth's first flowering plants to bloom across the landscape, encouraging insects to feed on their pollen and mammals and birds to spread their seeds. This led to a rapid rise in mammal and bird species until the new kings of the Earth crashed their way through the land. The meat eating territorial predatory dinosaur had arrived to keep the mammal population in check for another 75 million years. The snake survived what is believed to be a comet strike that killed off the large dinosaur 65 million years ago allowing a certain small mammal to become human. With far fewer dinosaur eggs for the snake to devour, it quickly took a liking to mammal flesh and blood. Mammals were easy prey for the serpent, easy to hypnotise and succumb to its venom, simple to swallow whole and digest in the gut.

Snakes are thought to have evolved from lizards during the middle Jurassic Period (174-164 million years ago). The original snake was a nocturnal, stealth hunting predator that had tiny hind legs with ankles and toes. The oldest fossil of a snake discovered is an Eophis underwoodi, a small serpent that lived in southern England, about 167 million years ago, discovered in a quarry near Oxford in 2015. The serpent is one of the oldest species of creature still living on our planet alongside its alligator cousin and deserves our respect. The snake has been around since the time of the dinosaur and to still be thriving in the era of humanity proves it is an adaptable, cunning creature who understands the way of nature and the natural forces of our planet. We may have grown in size from our early mammal existence millions of years ago, and the snake is much less of a threat to us today but it is still a creature to be aware of and on no account, ever underestimate the power of the serpent.

The serpent, along with the bull, dominated the early scene of the Anunnaki reign on Earth. According to the Sumerian creation tablets contained in the *Enuma Elish*, from out of the chaos born from the union of Tiamat, the Mother of Life, and Apsu, the Deep Expanse, a royal family of gods and goddesses were 'ordered' into creation for a purpose only known by Mummu who formed them from his creative energy into solid form. What in fact Mummu gave birth to was an eternal struggle between the first-born gods for the position of Lord of the universe and heir to Tiamat's 'Tablets of Destiny' that the goddess wore on her chest that allowed her to write the laws that governed the universe. She still dominated existence but her male children's frenzy for power worried her a little.

The creation texts reveal that the god Alalu, which translates as 'Waves', as of the sea, but could also mean vibration, was one of many gods to sit on the Nibirian throne of the mythological planet of Nibiru in the early stages. His name could imply that he stirred the oceans to create life, much like the Indian Lord Shiva who danced the world into life. And like Shiva, Alalu was associated with the serpent. For Alalu, it was his royal bloodline direct from the murky chaos of Mummu making him adaptable, cunning and resourceful. To reach his heavenly position as king of Nibiru, Alalu had assassinated the previous king; however, the serpent's reign only lasted for nine short years. Because of his failure to deal with a worsening warming climate, his cupbearer Anu, of the bull bloodline had reason to overthrow him. Anu, translates as Heaven.

The bull is much younger than the snake, only coming into existence during the Early Pleistocene period in the form of an auroch a mere two million years before the arrival of the Stone Age, 450,000 years ago. As was their tradition to settling conflicts, Alalu and Anu decided the crown by single combat with the winner taking all and the loser fleeing for his life. The defeated serpent fled to the only place he knew he would be safe from Anu's reach, the sacred planet of life that by order of the 'Tablets of Law', was a forbidden fruit and out of bounds to all gods and goddesses. Alalu knew the planet as Tiamat and we know it as Earth. From the safety of the sacred world, Alalu could plan how to regain his kingdom from the Bull of Heaven. First, the serpent had to lure him here.

Alalu knew that Anu loved gold more than anything in the universe. He loved all the shiny coloured stones that were made into jewellery and ceremonial tools, and to the serpent's delight, Earth was crammed full of them. Humanity were at the stage of Homo erectus when the gods arrived. The Babylonian texts calls these deities the Anunnaki, which means 'those from Heaven to Earth came, or literally, those from Anu to the Earth Mother came. Their arrival coincided with the moment in our history when we began forming certain stones into tools and weapons. Humanity were no longer one of the wild animals that followed the herd across the landscape in search for food from season to season. For a million years, Homo erectus ran with the wild beasts, scavenging the remains of a lion's dinner, left overs, but well worth fighting off the wolves and hyena's for. By sharpening flakes of rock, our ancestors rose up the food chain becoming in most instances, the hunter rather than the prey. Is it a coincidence that the Stone Age began at the same time the Anunnaki is said to have arrived on our planet?

Lord Anu did not need much persuading in sending a team to check the old serpent was not lying and when he was satisfied, teams of workers quickly followed to mine Tiamat's rich ores. When the mines were operational, Anu arrived on the sacred planet with his two eldest sons. The first-born was Enki, the god of water and proud son of his mother Antu, the sky goddess and sister of Alalu. Antu was the queen of the House of the Serpent bloodline. The mixed blood of the bull and serpent meant Enki could never have the right to sit in his father's throne. The heir to Anu's crown was Enlil, the god of the air whose mother was the Earth goddess, Ki, the sacred cow whose royal blood was as pure as the light of God himself.

At a ceremony for the King, Alalu cornered Anu and challenged the Bull of Heaven to another fight in single combat for the sacred throne of God on Earth and in Heaven. Anu had no choice but to accept the challenge made in front of his two sons and his royal attendants. It was a savage battle that went on for days before the serpent gained the upper hand crushing the breath out of Anu for all he was worth. He could sense victory as the bull fell limp, and released his grip a little. Then, the bull twists suddenly, moving himself in a position to bite off and swallow Alula's penis. In one lethal detachment, the serpent was denied an heir and any hope of kingship was gone forever. Alalu only had a daughter, the serpent priestess, Damkina. Her ambitions would have to wait, at least until Enki was ready for marriage.

The bull had won again. In fear for his life, the serpent fled to Mars to live among the Igigi who mined the red planet.

Enki grew up tormented by being the King's first born but only second in line to his younger brother for their father's crown. Enlil automatically inherited the position as head of the House of Bull so Enki, rather than become second to his brother again, chose to head the bloodline of his mother Antu as Lord of the Serpent Family. The princes each had a different outlook towards the human race. Enki saw us as having intelligence and capable of learning to work as a society to achieve great things. The serpent prince loved to teach humans, who began spreading into Europe during the Late Palaeolithic Period that began around 100,000 years ago when the continent was constantly gripped in continuous waves of severe ice ages. With the control of fire, butchering and sewing skills to make clothing and shelter from animal hide, humanity could now venture further into Europe for longer. Enki also opened the human mind to think for itself, have independent thought and ideas and make plans for the future in the development of the planet the Anunnaki called 'Mother of Life'; our Earth.

Enlil, on the other hand loved to hunt the many types of creatures of all shapes and sizes including the clever humans across the planet. As the heir to the throne, the sky god felt that all life on Earth were for his benefit and enjoyment. For Enlil, homo sapien were no different from the animals they hunted and sometimes hid from. Like the rest of life on our planet, humans were Enlil's prey and playthings to dominate and rule over.

Enki took Alalu's daughter Damkina as his queen, solidifying the power of the serpent household. Damkina became Ninki, Lady of the Earth. They had a son and heir that would achieve great power in the future, Marduk, which translates as 'Bull Calf'. Enlil made the wind goddess Ninlil his queen, producing the Moon god Sin as their heir to rule over the night sky.

Often overlooked in the Babylonian stories is the half-sister to both Enki and Enlil, the eldest daughter of Anu, the nature goddess Ninmah. She was just as ambitious as her two brothers were and had sons by both of them. Enki was the father of the rain god Ninurta and Enlil fathered the wind god Nergal. Ninurta took on the role as head of the House of the Lion and Nergal, the House of the Eagle. Like their half-brothers Marduk and Sin, they were second to none in their household.

When it was time to choose his successor, Enki had done enough to convince Anu that the old rules should not apply on Earth as it was a new enterprise and new laws were needed to be drawn up that favoured the first-born son of the King as his heir on the 'Mother of Life'. Enki the serpent became the Lord of the Earth and Enlil became the Lord of Command in charge of the King's vast army. The god of the air became ill with rage and vowed to disrupt his brother's plan to feed the human beings the fruit from the tree of knowledge.

The gods and goddesses on Earth became very noisy, quarrelsome, drunk, continuous partying and fighting soon broke the patience of Tiamat and Apsu who decided to punish them. Apsu and Mummu agreed the best action was to annihilate them all. They had become a plague on Mother Earth and needed eradicating. Tiamat was against that idea; she loved her children no matter what and warned Enki of what was coming. The serpent released a powerful spell that enchanted Apsu and Mummu into a deep sleep, took their powers and imprisoned them deep into the subterranean heart of the Earth Goddess. Tiamat was not happy about the loss of her great love and first-born son, and after some criticism for not retaliating from the children that lived in her realm outside of the chaos of space and time, the old Mother Goddess saw revenge as her best plan of action to retain her authority. Tiamat, now depicted as a demonised serpent gave birth to an army of demons and took the war to Earth.

It was a time for the serpent and bull on Earth to work together to defeat the 'She Dragon' that was coming their way. During council, it was agreed that whoever slew the angry Mother Goddess in single combat would inherit the Anunnaki crown on his return. Enki's son Marduk was an ambitious serpent and stood forward to accept the task of ridding the world of the aging grandmother goddess many millennia past her best. To prove he was a suitable candidate for the task, Marduk became invisible in front of the council and reappear again moments later. The young serpent knew a trick or two and had access to a good array of weapons to tackle the goddess with.

The battle was long and fierce but youth and strength was on the side of the prince and when the old goddess opened her jaws to devour the young upstart, Marduk, let loose a fiery arrow into her wide mouth, igniting the stomach gas of Tiamat and blowing her throat out. Before cutting her body in two, Marduk removed the Tablets of Destiny from the corpse of the goddess and placed them onto his own chest. The serpent now guided the destiny of the Earth and everything on her. With the world at his feet, Marduk wanted a queen to share it with. The serpent surprised everyone by taking a human bride. The most shocked and angry was his father Enki, seeing the royal bloodline of the serpent tarnished forever. Ninki quickly persuaded Enki to accept their son's wishes and take the Earth woman as the mother of his descendants. Marduk and Sarpanit gave birth to the messenger god Nabu who would be the perfect candidate to bring God's will to the human population.

With his queen, Ningal, the Bull of Sin fathered the trinity of Ereshkigal, the queen of the Underworld, Ishtar, the goddess of love and their young brother, the wise King Shamash, the prophet, and lawmaker for Earth.

It was not long before humanity spread to the four corners of the Earth, much to the dismay of Enlil, who set out a plan to wipe them off the face of the planet once and for all. It was time to cleanse the Earth goddess from the disease of humans poisoning her surface wherever they went. Enki discovered his brothers plan to flood the Earth and warned a favoured priest to construct an ark and save the essence of all living things on it.

The strength of the Bull merged with the determination of the Eagle when Nergal married his niece Ereshkigal, snatching control of the disembodied souls that constantly arrived into their underworld realm for the dead. The Eagle now governed the afterlife and became a symbol of the church with the domestication of the Bull to lead the flock to them. The cunning of the Serpent merged with the drive of the human feminine and mixed with the courage of Ninurta's Lion, became the symbol of the kings across Europe. The church worked with the crown to construct great city-states, supporting powerful armies allowing for expansion when required. Kings owned the human subject while the church owned their soul.

The human mind, once the safe domain of the Mother Goddess was now open to attack inside and out. When the Akkadians swept down on horseback from the north around 2,300 BCE under King Sargon I, the city of Babylon was established as the new administration centre for Mesopotamia. Many of the old Sumerian priests of Nabu migrated east to the Indus Valley and into India, taking the worship of their Bull with them.

A Serpent, a Bird and a Tree

There is a thread of an interaction between a serpent, a bird of prey and a tree weaving itself through the Sumerian and Babylonian texts and into other cultures too. One of the stories goes something like this.

A snake and an eagle were the best of friends, growing up together and becoming like family by the time they reached adulthood. They both decided to share a tree to live in when they grew up; the eagle perched at the very top in the canopy and the serpent at the very bottom amongst its roots. They were the very best of neighbours, and when they had families, they made an oath to guard over the others young from predators when they went to hunt for food. The set up worked for them both for years, having many children until something changed that destroyed their friendship forever. While the serpent was away hunting, the eagle swooped down destroying the snake's home and fed the baby serpents to his own chicks. There is no explanation as to why the eagle did this, but when the serpent returned to find his home wrecked and his babies gone, he was incandescent with rage and wanted revenge on his old friend for breaking their oath. When he climbed the tree, he found the eagle and his young had flown the nest. The serpent took his complaint to the sun god Shamash who revealed how to capture the bird, break its wings and leave it to suffer in a deep pit for eternity. Revenge was sweet for the scaly reptile.

Suffering much pain for what seemed an eternity, the eagle cried constantly to Shamash for help and when the sun god felt the bird had suffered enough and served its punishment, decided it was time to release it from the torment. The 14th king of Kish, from the root 'qosh' which means to lay bait or snare, Etana had shepherded a people in chaos and without guidance after the great flood, bringing order back into their lives, which suggests civilisation is much older than we are led to believe. To secure a permanence to his reign, Etana needed an heir but try as he might, was unable to produce a son. The king would offer daily sacrifices to Shamash for a boy. The sun god guided Etana to a mountain where he would find an injured eagle in a pit. If the king could save the bird, he would be guided to a magic herb that will ensure him a son. Etana found the suffering eagle and for half a year brought food and drink until the strength of the bird had recovered who promised the king he would carry him to the heavenly palace of Ishtar for the 'plant of birth'. A list of Sumerian kings recorded on a clay tablet has the name of Etana's son and successor Balih, suggesting his journey was a successful one.

A story from the Babylonian texts reveals a story of a serpent, a bird and a tree concerning the goddess of love, Ishtar and the demi god Gilgamesh, the king of Erech. Ishtar had taken a young huluppu tree, what experts have described as a kind of palm tree, from the banks of the River Euphrates and replanted it in her garden. From its timbers when it had matured, Ishtar wanted to make a bed and a throne but when it was ready to chop down, she found that a serpent had made a nest in its roots and a vulture with chicks roosting in its branches and both had refused to move. No matter what Ishtar did to try and get rid of them, they refused to budge and no amount of persuasion could move them. Frustrated and not wishing to harm them, the goddess of love called on her friend Gilgamesh to remove them for her. In gratitude, Ishtar gave him a magic drum and a drumstick made from the base and crown of the tree.

The Norse had a story of a serpent, a bird and a tree that includes a rodent stirring things up. At the centre of the Viking realm sits the world tree, an ash called Yggdrasil, Ygg, meaning Odin and drasil, horse. Odin's horse, or as scholars suggest, because

Odin hung himself from the tree, Yggdrasil means the 'horse of the hanged', or 'Odin's gallows'. Its roots were fed by waters from the three worlds, the bubbling waters of Hvergelmir in the underworld, the realm of the dead, the sacred well of Mimir in Midgard in the middleworld of humanity, and the fountain of Urd in the upperworld kingdom of the gods, Asgard.

Perched on its highest branch and keeping watch over the three worlds was the falcon Vedfolnir (Wind bleached) who reported all that he saw to Odin. Living amongst its roots was the serpent of Mimir, Jormungandr (Huge monster), the middle child of Loki between the eldest Hel, the goddess of death and Fenrir the wolf. The serpent was a powerful force of destruction and evil who gnawed constantly at the root that took its nourishment from the river Hvergelmir, hoping to kill the world tree knowing its death would trigger the downfall of the gods. Scampering between the branches and the base of Yggdrasil was a squirrel who passed on messages between the bird and the serpent called Ratatoskr (Drill tooth). The squirrel liked to spread gossip between the falcon above and the serpent below with the intention of making them both angry. Ratasoskr's relentless meddling caused Jormungandr to concentrate his attack on the tree root in the underworld with more and more venom bringing about Ragnarok.

At Ragnarok, when the Norse world ended, Hel escaped from her underground lair with her brother, Jormungandr, and her hellhound, Garm, to join Loki in the war against Asgard. After a long and bloody battle between the forces of good and evil, Asgard was finally defeated when Fenrir the wolf escaped his shackles and belched thick toxic smoke over the earth and Jormungandr flooded the world with one sweep of his giant tail bringing death and destruction to everything.

It is worth bearing in mind that this event was written down in the 'Prose Edda', compiled in the 13th century by Snorri Sturluson, an Icelandic historian, politician, poet and most tellingly a Christian. The reign of the Norse gods, goddesses and demons ended with the fire giant, Surtr, deciding to destroy everything with his flames except a man called Lifthrasir and a woman called Lif. When it was safe for them to do so, they emerged from the depths of Mimir's forest where they had fled when the world was set alight. They had remained in a deep slumber until the earth had regenerated itself signifying the arrival into the Biblical Garden of Eden as Adam and Eve.

A fascinating point was made in the book '*The Cygnus Mystery*', by Andrew Collins about a celestial serpent, bird and tree, in his search for the reason behind constructing early stone temples pointing towards the north. Thanks to the invention of the Skylobe computer programme, we can now see the heavens as they appeared in the ancient past. Interestingly, on the morning of the spring equinox of 15,000 BCE the stars that made up the constellation of the Serpent, later to be renamed Scorpio by the Greeks, appeared low on the eastern horizon before sunrise. The Milky Way flowed from the celestial serpent upwards to the celestial Vulture (Cygnus) that occupied the North Pole position at the time. This layout could have given birth to the concept of a world tree with a serpent at the base and a bird of prey sitting at the top of the 'trunk', of the Milky Way. At that time, the heavens circled the celestial bird that from the Earth, pointed the way to the place where it was believed the human soul was created and returned to after the death of the physical body.

The Hindu Serpent Gods

With the arrival of the Akkadians into Mesopotamia, a group of Sumerian priests not wishing to preach under Babylonian rule took their Bull religion eastwards following the foothills of the Himalayas to settle on the banks of the Indus Valley and into the Indian continent. From here, they would teach the local Neolithic hunter-gatherers the way of their gods and goddesses and civilise them to live in city-states much like they did back home. Creation for them began with the opposing feminine forces of Inanna and Ereshkigal, transforming them into Aditi (Infinity) and Diti (Finite). Aditi was the boundless heaven who embodied unlimited light and consciousness and depicted as the 'Sacred Cow of Heaven'. Diti was the dark serpent who constricted the world with her earthbound laws. Aditi was the mother of the Adityas, celestial deities who were the natural forces of the heavens. They regulated the movement of the sun, moon, planets and all the stars and the winds and waters that cleansed the earth. The children of Diti were the natural forces of the planet, the elemental dark demons that caused earthquakes and volcanic eruptions, all the negative events that occurred on Earth.

The sky god Varuna had created the world by picturing everything in his mind's eye. He possessed all knowledge and could control the destiny of humanity by initiating the will of his mother Aditi. The wind was his breath and the stars were his many eyes.

When a threat from the west arrived into India around 1,700 BCE, a great war broke out for control of the continent. This caused Varuna to strengthen his authority by absorbing all the separate powers of the Adityas into a single powerhouse of energy, a super god called Indra. The Hindu sagas of the Rig Vedas reveal Indra was born from heaven and earth, his father being the sky god Dyas, a red bull whose bellowing was the thunder and at night was seen as a black horse decked with pearls that represented the stars. Indra's mother was the earth goddess Prithivi who was depicted in the form of a cow and considered the source of all vegetation.

A prophecy warned that when Indra was born, he was destined to supplant the old order of gods, so his mother hid him away in a cave until he was old enough to look after himself. When he was old enough, Indra led the Devas, the gods and goddesses of light into battle against the Asura (Aryan) invaders, demonic serpents who possessed supernatural powers. The Devas were portrayed as uniting the universe bringing matter together in an orderly fashion where the aim of the Asuras was to separate and divide the world to create chaos. The serpents did all they could to deprive humanity of universal light of knowledge.

A young Indra freed a herd of cows that were stolen from the gods by demons and in doing so released the sacred force of the cosmos into the world. This allowed Indra to refashion the universe by measuring time by the sun and fixed four corner posts at each of the compass points between which he built the world walls. Above, Indra made a roof of clouds to shelter nature from the harsh glare from the sky. The wide doors of the world opened towards the east and every morning were opened to admit the sun. It was through these gates that the gods entered into the world to partake in sacrifices and libations. Indra created elves to fashion nature so that all creatures could feed from the 'Cow of Plenty'.

When the demons attempted to destroy nature, causing a famine to spread across the earth, Indra, with his twin brother Agni the fire god removed the curse and saved humanity. From that time on, the first fruits of the harvest were offered up to the gods. Both the Devas and Asuras were given life by the lord and master of all created beings, the protector god Prajapati, 'He who shines', who was the blueprint on which Brahma was created.

A wizard called Tvsahtri was determined to overthrow Indra, fathered a son called Trisiras who inherited his powers and had three heads, one to read the Vedas, one to perceive the world and one to eat with. He was very virtuous causing Indra to become concerned seeing Trisiras's popularity increase daily. Indra tempted the boy with beautiful young women to seduce him but nothing tempted him from his path of asceticism. Frustrated, Indra decided to strike him down with a thunderbolt. Even then, Trisiras continued to radiate a dazzling light over the entire world. To avenge his son, Tvsahtri created the demon serpent Vritra to challenge Indra to a fight to the death. Vritra was a fearsome serpent embodied with the dark and unproductive forces of nature, depriving humanity of the light of knowledge.

After many weeks of combat, the serpent managed to swallow Indra but the sky god was saved when the Devas prised Vritra's jaws apart allowing Indra to escape and resume the battle. After many more weeks, both gods become exhausted and with neither gaining an advantage agreed a truce. Vritra promised to make peace only if Indra ensured that he would not be killed with a weapon of iron, wood or stone, by anything wet or dry, or during the night or day, to which Indra agreed. In secret Vritra amassed an army of giants and demons that were so strongly armed they had become invincible and soon scattered the Devas in all directions. In an attempt to destroy nature, Vritra began to consume all the waters on earth and in the heavens leaving humanity, on the brink of extinction. One sunset, Indra came across a pillar of mist rising out of the sea, something not of iron or wood or stone. It was neither wet nor dry and being dusk, it was neither night nor day. Indra fashioned the pillar of mist into a thunderbolt and used it to split the serpent's stomach, releasing all the waters it had consumed and save the human race again.

Over time, the Asura forces were able to subdue the Devas and introduce new gods for the Indian people to make offerings and sacrifices to, the trinity of Brahma, Vishnu and Shiva. Indra and the Devas fled to reinvent themselves in Europe as Zeus and the Olympians.

As ever, the victors (re)write the history.

The priests of the new regime were religious leaders called Brahmins that preached of a trinity of gods radiating from a single cosmic energy called Brahman. They were the sole guardians of a sacred lore called the Rig Veda, a collection of Hindu hymns written between 1,500 and 800 BCE. It was an epic song of gods, goddesses and demons of an eternal cycle of creation, duration and destruction in the personalities of Brahma, Vishnu and Shiva.

Brahma was comprehended as the creator god bringing everything into being. He was often cast as the first of the gods, a personification of Brahman, the indestructible reality that exists in all things. Everything in the universe is a manifestation of Brahman and thus everything contains an element of the divine. Brahma is said to have sprung from a golden egg floating on the primeval waters of his creation.

Brahma desired that it should be so and he willed forth the principle of the universe; from this came the primal energy, and from that, the mind. Then there evolved the subtle elements and from these, the many worlds Mundaka Upanishad

Brahma corresponds to the birth process, producing all the material elements of the universe and the concepts that enables human beings to understand them. Some cast Brahma as the creative force of Vishnu, identifying the preserver god with Brahman, asserting that he had existed before anything else. Using his creative power (Maya) Vishnu created the vast primordial waters before resting on the 100-headed serpent called Ananta Shesha who represented eternity. In some stories, the naga Ananta Shesha represents the accumulated karma of the lives of those from the previous age, which determines the form of the next creation.

The root of the name Vishnu, 'vish' means to pervade. His main function is to ensure the triumph of good over evil. During his rest on the many headed world snake, Vishnu would slowly develop into another avatar. In his incarnation as Matsya the fish, Vishnu warned Manu, the first mortal man of a coming flood so he could make a ship to take the sages and the 'seeds of all existing things' to survive the deluge.

Vishnu maintains all things and has the power to manifest in many different forms. In the 'Great Cosmic Ocean', he reclines comfortably on the 'Serpent of Infinity' and is the primeval spirit of existence; the Lord of the Universe. Vishnu Purana

The purpose of Shiva is to destroy existence so that transformation can occur allowing something new and fresh to come into being to take its place. His name means 'Auspicious' and as 'Lord of the Dance', Shiva dances out the creation of the world. When he grows tired, Shiva relapses into inactivity causing the universe to return to chaos bringing destruction ending that cycle of existence.

Shiva is pure existence, pure consciousness, and a deity of the mind, master of the three worlds and the conqueror of death. The whole universe is created by the Shakti of Shiva. Shiva Purana

Shiva symbolises a deity within whom all opposing forces are reconciled. He is the penetrating power of focused energy spending much of his time meditating on Mount Kailas high in the Himalayas keeping the world in existence. He has four arms, a third eye in his forehead and rides an obedient milk white bull called Nandi. When visiting the rishis, the great sages of India, Shiva tried to persuade them to become his devotees but they cursed him. When that had no effect on him, the rishis sent a fierce tiger to devour him. Shiva simply removed its skin with his fingernail and draped it around his shoulders like a shawl. Then they sent a poisonous snake to kill him, but Shiva merely hung it around his neck as a scarf. Finally, they sent a dwarf with a club but Shiva responded by stepping on its back and danced on him. Admitting defeat, the rishis threw themselves at Shiva's feet and worshipped him.

In one tale from the Rig Veda, the great snake Vasuki was used as a rope to spin Mount Mandara back and forth in order to churn the cosmic ocean to produce the elixir of life, Amrita. Unfortunately, the snake became so exhausted he spewed his venom all over the ocean, which threatened to destroy all existence. To save the universe, Shiva swallowed the poison, which stained his throat blue.

Alongside Brahman was his wife Shakti, the Queen of Heaven, and the divine feminine energy of creation. Her name means 'Force, Power or Energy' and is the inner woman in both males and females. Without her, Brahma, Vishnu and Shiva would be powerless on this plane of existence. Shakti is the consort to all three of the major Hindu gods. As the wife of Brahma, she is Sarasvati, As Vishnu's wife she is Lakshmi and as Mrs Shiva, she is the triple goddesses of Parvati, Durga and Kali.

Sarasvati is the WORD of Brahma, his voice on Earth. Her name means 'Watery', and is the goddess of rivers and lakes. She bought fertility and wisdom into the world. Lakshmi is the goddess of beauty, wealth and good fortune and represents the universal mother. Parvati means 'Daughter of the Mountains', and is a gentle peaceful goddess and the mother of the god of wisdom and literature, the elephant headed Ganesha. Durga is the great mother goddess whose name means 'She who is difficult to approach', or 'Inaccessible'. Durga was said to have been born fully-grown and ready for battle. She is a brave and protective goddess. Kali, 'The Black One', is the personification of death and destruction and believed to have sprung from the forehead of Durga. Like her husband Shiva, Kali destroys in order for fresh things to exist in the physical realm.

Brahma, Vishnu and Shiva grew out of the old Indian gods of Indra (sky), Agni (fire) and Yama (death). They were also the blueprint for the Greek brothers Zeus, Poseidon and Hades. From the very beginning, three has been a powerful number representing the universal law of life, death and rebirth. The triple energies represent the three elements of Fire, Water and Air with humanity being Earth and the combination of the other three. Fire sits at the very top and is the creative spirit of the universe residing in the kingdom of the soul. Below is Water who understands the intention of Fire from the realm of the heart. Air sits below Water putting into action the will of Fire into the palace of the mind. In other words, the highest energy of the universe is transmitted into the receptive processing force to 'translate' if you like an interpretation the human mind can understand. These three forces regulate everything that happens in the world.

To be able to connect and interact with these powers we need to understand the process of the serpent energy known as Kundalini.

The Kundalini

Also known as the cosmic serpent, the inner woman and Shakti energy, kundalini is a powerful latent force residing at the base of the spine that can be aroused through various methods including meditation, yoga, dancing and tantric sex. This normally sleeping force, when awakened ascends through the central channel of the astral body to the crown of the head. The root word 'kunda' means 'pool' or 'reservoir of energy and is likened to a coiled snake ready to strike at any moment. When it is correctly directed, it can cause cosmic consciousness to manifest throughout your being and freedom from the physical body can be achieved.

A very important factor in achieving kundalini is the awareness of breath. Breath is life and something we generally take for granted and yet it is possibly the most vital aspect of our being. If the breath can be controlled, the mind can be stilled and bring calm to the fundamental forces in the body. An immediate effect is experienced with a feeling of an increase in energy, inner peace and calmness, the senses are turned up and you are able to function more effectively. To control the breath, first you have to be aware of the natural division of the breathing process, the in-breath, retention and out-breath.

The in-breath should be natural and not forced; air should flow into the body as a result of the expansion of the abdomen. When the breath is retained, the stomach should take the shape of a pot. The retention of breath is the point of greatest potency. During this period, the inhaled air is partly absorbed by the lungs, vitalising the whole body. The outbreath rids the system of waste gases and energies.

Tantric teaching advises that during inhalations you should imagine absorbing the life giving energies of Brahma. There is no reason I can think of to imagine absorbing the god or goddess energy you are familiar with. During retention, you should focus extracting the life force of the air circulating through the whole body in the blood. Conscious retention strengthens the circulation and reinforces the subtle connections among all parts of the body. During exhalation, you should imagine all negativity, physical ailments and tensions leaving your body. These three parts of the breathing process should interact smoothly. There are many different techniques available suggesting lengths of retention time, nose or mouth inhalation and exhalation that are worth researching yourself.

The tantras is a spiritual method of being fully immersed with the Shakti energy, taking into account both inner and outer realities, getting our spiritual and physical selves working together. It teaches various ways for awakening and channelling the kundalini energy. The primordial feminine energy of the cosmos 'sleeps' in the sexual regions of the body in the form of a coiled snake. As long as she remains asleep, the individual soul, the essence of a person is limited and true knowledge cannot be gained. The conscious awakening and control of kundalini requires strength of mind, the awareness of the evolutionary upward movement of the raw sexual energy and a physical body in harmonious balance.

Sexual contact is generally enough to awaken the cosmic serpent within. Lovers experience kundalini through the natural act of lovemaking, the deep breathing, rhythmic movement, the exchange of vital breaths and bodily fluids and (for some) the cries of passion in the throes of ecstasy. These are all factors that play a role in stimulating the serpent power. It offers the couple a great opportunity to explore the heights the inner spirit can reach.

Visualise the coiled kundalini in both yourself and your partner. Lead Shakti lovingly through her journey up through the spine opening the chakras along the way. Lead her in union from the sexual region up to the crown of your head and flood your hearts with the blissful energy of Shakti and Shiva. Visualise the kundalini as a sensuous woman, an extremely beautiful goddess filled with sexuality. She is ever willing and able to transport you to the individual heights of cosmic oneness. Think of her often, talk to her and always try to please her and she will grant you fulfilment. On her journey towards the heavens, Shakti passes through activating the seven main chakras up the spine causing them to open and vibrate. The higher the chakra point is up the body, the faster it vibrates until it matches the frequency of her lover Shiva when the serpent of Shakti becomes at one with him.

There are seven main chakras that spin and glow a certain colour when activated, each one governing a different part of the human conditioning. Starting at the most dense and lowest vibrating chakra that connects us to the spirit of Mother Earth is the root chakra. It is here that the serpent sleeps, coiled in the quiet of her nest in the roots of a mature tree. The root chakra deals with survival and the awareness of any immediate danger, this chakra can become blocked by fear. When it is activated, it shines red and is associated with the planet Saturn (Kronos & Ninurta). Once the root chakra has opened, the serpent uncoils and moves up the spine (the tree) into the base of the abdomen to awaken the sacral chakra. This point of power is associated with pleasure and blocked by guilt. It glows orange when activated and is governed by the planet Mars (Ares & Nergal). The serpent continues up the spine to the diaphragm to ignite the solar plexus chakra. Here will power resides, a gift from the goddess, becoming blocked by shame. When it is open, the chakra glows yellow and is influenced by the planet Jupiter (Zeus & Marduk). Next, the serpent arrives at the half way point at the centre of the upper body in the heart chakra. The heart is love and its radiance can spread that love out to all the other chakras. The heart chakra can be blocked by grief. It emanates a green light, the colour of nature and of Mother Earth and fed by the warmth and light of the Sun (Helios/Apollo & Shamash).

From love, the serpent, whose tail is still 'earthed' in the root chakra, unwinds further to glide into the throat chakra that can reveal the truth of the universe and blocked by lies. It radiates a deep blue and is influenced by the planet of love Venus (Aphrodite & Ishtar). From the throat, the serpent races into the head at the top of the spine in the centre of the brain. The pineal gland or more commonly known as the third eye chakra brings insight and blocked by illusion. It shines indigo and is associated with the 'Great Lady', our Moon (Artemis & Sin). Then comes the bite, the serpent has found her mark at the top of the head and her mergence into the primordial universal spirit. Shakti has found Shiva, the body has found bliss and the Earth is connected to the rest of the universe. The dazzling violet glow of the crown chakra feeds the soul with cosmic energy and blocked by ego attachment. Its influencing planet is tiny Mercury (Hermes & Nabu), the solar system's closest planet to our star and fastest orbiting. Mercury, better known as the Greek messenger god Hermes was the son of Zeus and the Pleiad nymph Maia, flew across the sky with wings on his sandals, fought his enemies using his helmet of invisibility and carried a caduceus, a rod with two spiralling serpents around it, with a pair of eagle wings at the top.

Once the crown chakra has activated, the physical realm is seen for the illusion it is and the spiritual realm for the truth it is. The serpent, who sits in both realms, is the conduit between heaven and earth, humanity and the god and goddess.

There are many ways to enhance the experience of the kundalini rising through the body to connect with the spirit world; it is not just about sex. Simple things like natural earth sounds, listening to streams and waterfalls, rain on the window, the blast of thunder and flash of lightning can be enough to stir the serpent into wakefulness. Who is not moved by the intricate warble of birdsong? I am not sure human laughter can be classed as a natural earth sound, but it should be.

Indian yoga is largely based on an eight-step guide to

perfection. The first step and probably the most difficult in my opinion, concerns discipline, meaning controlling the urge to retaliate over anything that annoys you. It is about being able to walk away from confrontation and treating others as you would like to be treated yourself, soul to soul. The first step is mainly taking control of your mind, think before reacting to anything and respect other people's opinions and beliefs. They have souls too. Step two is being of good heart and be content with all the good in your life. It is mainly about finding your way on the path towards understanding and righteousness. First, you have to subdue the bullying ego into working for you and not itself, now there is a challenge. The third step is keeping the body and mind healthy and working together, the heart and head in unison. Things like yoga, martial arts, tai chi, anything that focuses the mind on the relationship of the body and breath of our being. The fourth step concerns the control of vital energy through breathing which we have already covered. The fifth step is the disassociation of the outside world and the exploration of the inner realm without mind. It is having no sense of space and time, no thoughts or feelings, being without any outside influence. The sixth step concentrates on mindfulness, being mindful of your actions and reactions and to be watchful of what you say to others. The seventh step is using meditation to stir the coiled serpent at the base of the spine into action, which is not only sitting still with your eyes closed and emptying the mind. Witnessing a beautiful sunset, watching the stars, dancing, listening to inspiring music, creating art, being in nature, in a forest, gardening, whatever your passion is and fully engaging with it is a form of meditation. Being in the zone as they say. Anything that induces being in the zone is meditative; anything that focuses the mind in an act of pleasure will awaken the sleeping serpent into activity. Step eight is Samadhi, the Hindu word for the super conscious state, when Shakti holds her beloved

The Serpents of the Pharaohs

While the forces of the serpent and bull played out in Mesopotamia and India, a third mighty empire existed along the fertile River Nile in Kemet, better known as Egypt today. Here, they also had a great rivalry between the opposing forces of the serpent and bull influencing their world. Their myths changed regularly depending who ruled at the time. There are many versions of the creation myths as there was with all their stories concerning the gods and goddesses before the time of the pharaohs.

The early Egyptians saw their world as three different realms, the Earth, the sky and the Duat, or underworld and surrounded by the waters of chaos. Their world began with a single mound that rose from the primordial waters of creation, which contained the cosmic energy that was the source of all life. The first god to materialize was Atum, 'he who came into being by himself'. He created his children, the twins Shu, the air god and Tefnut the water goddess by masturbating them into existence, forming our planet's atmosphere. Shu and Tefnut produced the earth god Geb and the sky goddess Nut. Geb and Nut in turn gave birth to the opposing forces of Osiris and Seth and their respective consorts, Isis and Nephthys. From these origins, all other life came into being.

When his offspring drifted away, Atum became lonely, so removed one of his eyes, filled it with some of his power and elevated it to the status of a goddess, his daughter who manifested as the twin personalities of Hathor and Sekhmet. Hathor was a milk cow goddess of fertility and love while Sekhmet was blessed as a goddess of war with the head of a lioness on which was crowned with a solar disc and the uraeus (royal) serpent. Atum then commanded the goddess to track down his children and return them to him. Eventually, Shu and Tefnut were found and unable to contain his joy, Atum wept uncontrollably. His tears fell to the earth and transformed into the first human beings. Atum was so happy; he placed the 'Eye of Hathor-Sekhmet on his forehead in the form of a cobra so she would be feared by gods and men alike.

The masturbating creator god became too provocative for the later high priests and merged him with the sun god Re. The creational duties were passed onto Ptah who brought the universe into being simply by thought and word, much like Varuna did in India.

In the heart of Egypt, the Ogdoad, or 'Group of Eight', consisted of four pairs of male and female deities who inhabited the primeval waters before the world existed. The males were in the form of frogs that represented fertility, order and rebirth, and the females were snakes representing the forces of elemental chaos like earthquakes and storms. The gods and goddesses were paired to represent the four different aspects of the universe before the world was formed. Nun and his consort Naunet together personified the original formless ocean. Heh and Hauhet were the infinity of the universe. Kek and Kauket embodied the darkness of night, and Amun and Amaunet were the dual incarnation, the opposing powers of the universal energy of life. Over time, the pairs merged into single gods before merging again to become the super god Amun.

To solidify the power over all of Egypt, a composite God with Atum-Re as the face, Ptah as the body and Amun as the light of creation, came into being.

Serpents have been largely represented as elemental symbols of chaos and evil throughout Egypt's history. It reflects the real danger from their deadly venomous bite. To minimise the risk of being bitten, Egyptians wore magic amulets. In Lower Egypt however, the snake had a positive connotation and symbolised by its patron, the goddess Wadjet. The cobra goddess Renenutel, whose name means 'the nourishing snake', was the goddess of good fortune and was invoked to ensure bountiful harvests, easy childbirth and a happy future.

The apocalypse, or the revealing of the truth, was believed could be brought about by the great serpent Apophis who lay in wait to attack the sun Re each night during his journey through the underworld. The forces of darkness, embodied in the god Apophis represented the source of all evil and the creator of chaos. His birth came about when the archer goddess Neith spat into the primeval waters of Nun. Apophis literally means 'he who was spat out'. Neith was born from the tears of Atum-Re and was the mother of the sun, but his radiance was so dazzling he could not see his mother and began to cry, his tears creating humanity. Neith found that goodness and light could not exist alone so evil and darkness in the form of a great serpent was born.

Apophis was the opposing force and nemesis of the sun and the embodiment of the forces of chaos that churned within Nut's ocean. His huge serpentine coils slithered in the Duat in the realm of the dead where the soul went after judgement. Every evening Apophis waited for Re to journey through and tried to prevent him from passing and rising the next morning. For protection, a serpent called Mehen coiled around the sun god during his journey through the night. Re overcome Apophis with the aid of spells and magic. His victory over the serpent every night was considered vital to the continued existence of all life on the planet. If Apophis ever did defeat Re, the world (as we know it) would end. By defeating the serpent each night allowed the sun god to rise every morning to take his rightful place sailing across the sky in his boat as a sign and guarantee of cosmic security. Even after sunrise, Apophis would sometimes raise storm clouds to diminish the light of Re. In temples across Egypt, priests conducted rituals to assist Re on his journey through Duat. Prayers were offered, incantations chanted and magic spells performed using the secret names of Apophis. They were written in ink on papyrus and burned. Also, in some instances, wax images in the form of serpents were ceremoniously spat on, mutilated and set alight to ward off disaster. Solar eclipses provoked fear into the population believing Re had been swallowed whole the previous night and only the magic of the priests could revive him.

However, it was just as important that Apophis could not be ultimately destroyed or the balance between the forces of good and evil would be altered and the world would be plunged into the darkness from where it had come.

The Mother Goddess Isis, wife and sister of Osiris wished to place her family at the head of the pantheon of gods that ruled Egypt and the only way she could achieve that was to discover the secret name of Re that would give her some real power over the universe. To do that, Isis had to be very clever and a little bit cunning. She had been born with the power of the serpent and as a fiery and protective goddess, she often took the form of a cobra, representing the solar power of God and associated with the 'Eye of Re' (Hathor-Sekhmet).

When Isis came across Re sleeping, she noticed a long dribble of saliva drop from the corner of his mouth. She scooped it up, mixed it with clay and formed it into a poisonous snake. Then, with a little of her own magic, she breathed life into the effigy and left it at a crossroad she knew the sun god would take on one of his regular walks. When the snake bit Re, he felt the venom course through his whole body, causing him extreme pain. He asked the other gods to help but none of them could do anything and began to mourn the impending loss of the sun. Isis offered to cure him in return for his secret name but Re refused. Several times Re refused her help until he was in so much agony, he agreed to reveal his true name on the condition she disclosed it to no one else. Isis accepted his terms, and speaking out the god's secret name, she removed the poison, healing Re immediately. Isis and her family attained the power she craved.

It is worth mentioning the Egyptian myth concerning a serpent, a bird and a tree. On the sun's first ever rising over the land of Kemet, it rose in the form of a sacred bird called the Benu, possibly a grey heron, perhaps a yellow wagtail. It roosted in the branches of the tree of life, the sacred persea tree of the laurel family, which has solar significance. The sacred tree was protected from destruction from the cosmic serpent Apophis, also known as Apep, the opponent of light and order, by the 'Great Cat', of Re. The sun god's cat was the sun goddess of war, Mau, 'Felis catus', a black spotted ginger cat who prevented Apep of taking control of the persea tree which would give him the dominance over the sun. By cutting off his head with a flint knife, the serpent was banished to the underworld to constantly battle Re during his journey through the night.

When Re relinquished his rule on Earth and went to reside in the heavens, he left as his successor his son Shu who was succeeded by his son Geb and in turn his son Osiris. The younger brother of Osiris, Seth was jealous of the god's power and prestige, and plotted to overthrow him. Seth decided it was time to act when he discovered his wife Nephthys had a child, the ibis headed Anubis, with his hated rival Osiris. It pushed Seth over the edge with only murder on his mind. One story reveals how Osiris was trampled to death by Seth in the form of a bull only to be restored back to life by Isis. If Seth was going to kill his brother, he would have to be more cunning to ensure Isis could not resurrect him again. At a party with some of the gods, Seth tricked Osiris into a chest, sealed it tight and threw it into the Nile. Seth told the assembly of gods that Osiris had gone on a walk about in the wilderness and was not coming back and claimed his throne. When Osiris failed to return, the worst was feared and Seth was made king of Egypt safe in the knowledge that his brother left no heir to challenge him for his crown. Isis was not convinced and made plans to search for her husband causing Seth to recover the corpse of Osiris, hack his body to pieces and scatter them across Egypt. He did not count on the determination of Isis who, with her sister, Nephthys, scoured the land using all her magic, to find all of the pieces of her husband and stitched them all together. By calling out Re's secret name, Osiris is resurrected long enough to impregnate Isis with an heir, the falcon headed Horus. She hid him away until he was of an age to take on Uncle Seth, Horus was cared for and wet nursed by the cow headed Hathor.

When she was prepared, Isis took her son before the assembly of gods demanding the birthright of Horus of his father's kingdom. The council was divided on who they felt was most suitable to rule Egypt and decided the pair should fight it out in single combat with the victor winning the crown of heaven. They had some interesting battles using cunning, strength, magic and a little help from some of the other gods and goddesses that went on for eighty decades. During one battle, Horus chopped off Seth's fore leg when he was a bull and flung it into the night sky where it hung as the constellation the 'Great Bear', or 'Plough'. In another battle, Horus lost one of his eyes and although it was restored, he gave it to his father and replaced it with the all-seeing, all knowing divine serpent, which acted as the emblem of authority on the crowns of all the pharaohs that followed.

Horus had revenge as his goal and Seth had ego as his drive. The conflict between the two gods represents the forces of order against the forces of chaos and confusion. With order came the certainty that required a hierarchy with God at the top, the workers at the bottom and a host of power men like kings and priests, merchants and business owners in between. With chaos came societies without laws and control, without layers of officialdom between the population and God. As fate would have it Horus won and Seth was adopted by Re to join him on his solar boat to become thunder in the sky by day and Re's protector from Apophis in the underworld at night.

The successors of Horus were the pharaohs, the god kings of Egypt who had absolute power on Earth, who built the pyramids and held the people of Moses in captive as slaves. When a pharaoh died, he was mummified to take the form of Osiris after he was pieced together by Isis and was believed to become Osiris himself. Power has to flow for it to work, everything had to be replaced and renewed for the world to evolve. From (Re)birth to king, from king to god and from god to the rest of the universe, shedding his skin at each level.

Dreamtime Serpent

Joondalup Lake was within easy walking distance from my brother's house, so rather than a booze cruise up Swan River with my family, I chose to have an adventure around Yellagonga Regional Park instead. Named after the chief of the Moora Nyunger people who inhabited the region north of the Swan river before the Europeans arrived. Our mum had treated me, my sister and brother to a three-week holiday in Perth, Western Australia, staying with our youngest brother, his wife and two crazy dogs. It was a holiday of a lifetime, financed by mum and my spending money coming from the sale of an old motorbike I had. It was a good time to escape Britain's chill of early March. We could guarantee three weeks of sunshine and heat, 20°C which we found hot, but for the Australians it felt cold because the week before our arrival they were basking in temperatures double that. It was as if we bought the cold with us, which suited me, I am not a great fan of heat. Back home we were just coming into spring with the goddess Bridget working her magic to reawaken nature once more. Here, on the other side of the world, autumn was about to fall and the Australian version of the barren Cailleach was about to bring darkness and less warmth to the landscape, putting most of nature to sleep. I was reliably informed the snakes at this time of year were more than likely sleeping off a busy summer.

I pretty much had the place to myself and in only a t-shirt, shorts, and a pair of espadrilles and armed with my camera, I ventured into the depths of the undergrowth off the path that surrounded the lake. I could feel the ancient energy of the creator serpent Wagyl and the primal energy of the nature spirits that resided here. The town that surrounded the lake, Joondalup was less than twenty years old, constructed as part of the expansion of Perth whose city centre was thirty miles south from here.

Apart from a tarmacked path and some wooden jetties into the lake, the earth spirits here had largely been undisturbed.

For a sense of understanding of the country, I read 'Songlines', (1987) by Bruce Chatwin before I left the UK. He described how aborigines walked the songlines, sacred places along a path of creation that could be activated to reveal the energy of that place during dreamtime when the land itself was formed.

Inside the canopy of the trees and bushes, I felt connected to the land and a sense of respect that the aborigines had with Mother Earth. I could also feel an undertone of fear and suffering when civilization from Europe reached here and hunted inhabitants down like wild animals for fun.

I was bought out of my thoughts by a cyclist on the path beckoning me to him. Like myself, the cyclist was a photographer, a local wildlife and nature photographer called Gary Tate, who often cycled the path around the lake to photograph the wild life and assured me that not all snakes were in hibernation. Serpents rely on vibrations in the ground as a warning of unexpected visitors. They could feel a walker getting closer from a hundred paces, giving them plenty of time to slither to safety. A cycle tyre is less easy to detect meaning a cyclist is more likely to come across a basking snake on the path, perfect for a wildlife photographer. He had photographed a tiger snake only an hour earlier not far from this spot and to be wandering around in the long grass was foolhardy. I could have quite easily have stood on one. Tiger snakes are one of the most poisonous snakes in the world and if I were bitten by one, without a serum, would be dead in about three minutes. I kept to the trail after that.

The aboriginal creation story was passed on from word to mouth for thousands of generations, enacted in song, ritual and dance, paintings on tree bark and etched on rock. It was a piece of the puzzle connecting the old gods and goddesses with their animal connections representing the balancing of the earth and heavenly energies, the earth serpent and cosmic bovine. It is the interaction of these powers that drives humanity forward into the future. For Apophis to constantly battle with Re was the same as the serpent fighting with Indra or Enlil or romancing the goddess of love Ishtar. It could just as well be good versus evil, light versus dark, positive versus negative, 1 versus 0 and so on.

The significance of the opposing dualities is symbolically interwoven with the figure of the serpent whose venomous bite can bring a painful death or cure a painful ailment. The serpent is represented on rock and cave walls all across the Australian continent. Its slender shape reminded the early Australian people of a rainbow associated with much needed life giving rain.

Dreamtime explains the reason for the many animal bloodlines that ruled the first three major empires of Asia and Africa. At the heart of the Australian creation story is a snake, the Rainbow Serpent. The Rainbow Serpent was the creator goddess, the giver of life and associated with the fresh waters of rain, rivers and lakes. Before the Earth had formed and nothing moved or grew, the Rainbow Serpent slept below the surface, resting between activities. Then she woke, wriggled and stretched, thrusting her way up through the ground into a fresh new world ready to be designed, sparking into existence dreamtime. This was the period aborigines saw as the world coming into existence by the raw energy of earth's spirits. For the first settlers of Australia, the land was as much spiritual as it was physical.

Rainbow Serpent wriggled her way across the Earth, gouging out ravines and pushing up mountains. Then she woke the frogs up, with their bellies full with water they had stored during their hibernation. When Rainbow Serpent tickled their full stomachs, making them laugh, they spewed their water out all over the land, filling the tracks made by the serpent. With fresh water on the Earth, grass, bushes and trees grew, waking up all the animal spirits that lived in nature joining the serpents roaming the land. Kangaroos, wallabies, lizard's crocodiles and a host of other animals made their mark on the landscape, giving it a sacred significance.

From high up among the stars, the Numbakulla brothers, powerful gods took an interest in our planet and searched it to see what secrets she held. Almost overlooked, the brothers noticed in a shadow of a rock, in the wet clay, a jelly like unformed substance. Despite having short limbs, the jelly lacked all power of movement and had no physical senses to allow any social interaction with one another. Feeling they should help the poor deaf, dumb and blind creatures, the brothers descended to the Earth and cut them free from the sticky mud in the shape of humans. Then they gave them organs and senses and divided them into males and females so they could reproduce themselves. All they required was a spirit to fill them.

All the animal spirits got on fine for a time, then some began causing trouble and fighting with the other animals. To keep them all under control, Rainbow Serpent made laws with those that obeyed would be rewarded with a human form and those that disobeyed would be turned into mountains and hills and never walk the Earth again. Each obedient animal spirit that became human were given the title of the animal, bird or reptile that they transformed from. They formed tribes recognising each other by their totems, the kangaroo, the emu, the snake etc. Rainbow Snake ruled that no person should eat their totem animal; this way there would be enough food for everyone. The tribes lived together peacefully on the land given to them by Rainbow Serpent with the understanding it would always belong to them.

The original life force of the animal spirits remain embedded within the earth spirit allowing following generations to reconnect with the lands creation. Aborigines could draw on their ancestor's primal energy, strength and skill by coming into contact with a certain stone, bush or river that had significance and meaning to them. Australians first citizens knew every inch of their ancestral territory. With the right rituals, Aborigines today can still connect to the moment of creation when Earth's spirit formed our planet, when the dream resonated across the landscape.

Rainbow Serpent was called by different names by the many tribes spread across the continent. A black rock-snake called Kurrichalpongo answering a prayer to a northern tribesman that had been mocked and deceived by his fellow clan, bored a hole in the bank of a billabong, releasing a deluge that flooded the whole area. His tribe who were not swept away transformed into birds and flew away or turtles who simply swam away. Kurrichalpongo rested a while to lay eggs, which hatched into baby Rainbow Snakes and spread across the whole continent forming more rivers and lakes as they went.

At another place nearby, Kurrichalpongo suddenly reared upwards with her eyes flashing and tongue flicking, caused the skies to grow black with storm clouds. Thunder and lightning rumbled over the land causing mountains to crumble and the Earth to quake. Fierce winds uprooted trees and a torrent of rain flooded the banks of rivers carrying away everything in its path.

Around Perth and most of South Western Australia was created by a water snake called Wagyl who it is said was both male and female and simultaneously one serpent and many. The snake god Taipan could not only control human life and death but could also control thunder and lightning. Taipan is seen as the red spectrum of the rainbow. The serpent Ngalyod swallowed three birds who pecked their way out of the snake's stomach, emerging as three wise men.

The Kuniya or rock python people lived in the desert in peace with their neighbours. Harmonious as it was, the rock python craved excitement and adventure, new places to explore and live. They found a spot not too far away from their friends for comfort but far enough away to deter casual visitors. They lived peacefully and fruitfully for many generations until a tribe of deadly Liru, the venomous people of the carpet snake swept suddenly onto the rock python camp. A great battle followed causing the ground to rumble and give way through all the vibrations the serpents generated fighting each other. All that remained at the end of the battle was the great red rock known as Uluru. Uluru's appearance marked the end of the creative actions of dreamtime. The laws of the universe were fixed in place with the spirits in human form stuck in human bodies and those in animal form remaining as animals for the rest of time. Earth and nature was in perfect balance between humanity, nature and all of the animals for thousands of years until the European bull discovered Australia in 1770 and made it their own.

O Serpentis Graeca et Keltoi

According to the Greeks, history began with them. Everything that went before was merely chaos that needed to fade into the mists of time. The serpent to them was a force of darkness and evil and had to be destroyed at all costs. The wisdom of the serpent was reserved for the rich and powerful that joined the many secret societies and mystery cults that were popular throughout Greece at the time.

An early creation myth describes how Gaia was born spontaneously from chaos. Finding no ground to stand on, Gaia created the ocean and danced on the waves, stirring up the wind from which a giant serpent was formed. Then the goddess transformed into a dove and laid a huge egg, which the serpent (sperm) fertilized, from which everything in the universe was hatched. Two of the earliest gods to come into existence were the Titans Phorcys and Ceto, a primordial sea god and goddess who gave life to the goddess Echidna. Echidna was a beautiful woman from the waist up with a hideous serpent tail from the waist down. She lived alone in a cave in Pontus on the southern coast of the Black Sea *'beneath the secret parts of the holy earth'* carrying off unwary passers-by to feed on.

When war broke out between the Titans and the Olympians, Gaia, with the god of darkness and the underworld, Tartarus, gave birth to the monster serpent, Typhon, to fight against Zeus in his war against the giants. With the goddess Echidna, Typhon fathered many children to help the Titans cause, including the three-headed hellhound, Cerberus, who guarded the gates of the underworld, the fire breathing Chimaera who was part lion, part serpent and part goat and the sphinx who had the head of a woman and the body of a lion. With a 100 heads, Typhon was a formidable opponent against Zeus who agreed to fight him in single combat. At one point, it looked as if the serpent had won when he managed to cut out the tendons of Zeus's hands and feet and hid them leaving the god of the air disabled and unable to continue. Coming to the rescue of his father, Hermes found the tendons and restored them allowing Zeus to resume his battle with Typhon. Gradually, Zeus was able to wear down the serpent and drove him out of Greece into Italy, imprisoning him in the depths of Mount Etna.

The half human, half serpent, Echidna, was the sister of the Gorgons, three stunningly beautiful women, Stheno (strength), Euryale (far leaping) and Medusa (queen). While giving offerings in the temple of Athena, Poseidon arrived and unable to resist the beauty of Medusa, raped her leaving the goddess distraught and disgusted. Seeing her temple defiled, Athena was livid and jealous of her good looks, blamed Medusa for tempting the god of the sea to act the way he did. Athena, the goddess of wisdom and war punished Medusa by transforming her into a snake haired monster that turned any man that set eyes on her into stone. For standing by her sister, Stheno and Euryale shared the same fate forcing all three of them into exile on an island at the western extremes of the known world keeping out of sight of any prying eyes.

The most important oracle in the whole of Greece was the shrine at Delphi on the slopes of Mount Parnassus. Delphi was seen as the centre of the Greek world and regarded as the 'naval of the world' after Zeus placed a marble sacred stone known as the omphalos to mark its importance. The shrine had been guarded for millennia by the monstrous serpent Python, an earth spirit who had been sent by his mother Gaia to protect the priestess Pythia who prophesised the destinies of royalty and rich merchants who visited the site. When the god of light, Apollo, discovered the sacred place, he killed Python with a volley of 100 arrows, took possession of the oracle and made it his own. According to Delphic myth, it was the fumes that rose from the rotting corpse of the serpent that the oracle inhaled causing her to fall into a prophetic state.

Herakles, better known by his Roman name Hercules was a son of Zeus and a mortal woman called Alcmene. Hercules was born with great strength but also a vicious temper to go with it, which made him someone to be wary of. Zeus tricked his wife Hera into breast-feeding his baby son on her milk of immortality so Hercules would grow up to be a god. When Hera discovered the deception, she sent two poisonous vipers to kill the baby as he slept but discovered the young Hercules had killed the snakes and was playing with their dead bodies as toys. Hera never forgot the deception and when Hercules was grown up and happily married with children, she struck again. Hera cast a spell causing Hercules to become insane and believing his children were demons, killed them. When the madness wore off, realising what he had done, decided to seek redemption at Apollo's oracle at Delphi. The priestess instructed Hercules to atone for his sin by performing a number of tasks for his cousin, Eurystheus, the king of Mycenae. Eurystheus saw Hercules as a threat to his crown so gave the demi-god twelve 'impossible' labours in the hope one of them would kill him off.

After disposing of the Nemean lion, Hercules then had to slay the mighty nine-headed water snake, Hydra, at her lair on Lake Lerna. Hydra was another offspring of Echidna and

Typhon and a formidable opponent for Hercules who was accompanied by his friend, Iolaus, for company. Luring Hydra to the mouth of her lair, Hercules began to smash her heads with his club, but out of each crushed head, two fresh ones grew in its place. Even using his sword, new heads appeared from the fresh cuts. Thinking on his feet, Hercules called on Iolaus to pass him the lighted torch to sear the neck each time he cut off a head stopping new heads from growing until only one head remained. Athena warned Hercules that this remaining head was immortal and could not be killed so Hercules sliced off the final head and buried it beneath a great boulder, trapping it in the earth so it was no threat to anyone again. Hydra was dead. Hercules went on to complete his remaining labours, freeing himself from his guilt and shame to venture into the future, battling injustices and enemies to his heart's content.

The Greek gods, demi-gods and heroes managed to kill off any support for the serpent across most of Eastern Europe apart from those associated with the dark goddess Hekate. The 'distant one' was known as the 'Guardian of the Serpent Power', and the 'Queen of Demons' and popular with modern day witches. She had many sacred animals like the dog and horse but favoured the serpent for her prophecies and bringing spirits up from the underworld to do her bidding. Many snakes lived in her garden that she used for divination and summoning spirits. Her serpents were powerful harbingers of higher forces into the material plane.

Hekate was the daughter of the Titans Perses and Asteria and was the goddess of all nature, often depicted as wearing serpents on her girdle and usually seen in the presence of snakes. Hekate used snakes in rituals for fertility, protection and success and their venom as medicine to cure a number of ailments. The spirits she resurrected from the dead often appeared as snakes. When Hekate met a soul on the sacred crossroads between this world and the next, she was generally crowned with wild serpents and oak leaves, symbols of nature and fertility.

The Romans absorbed the Greek gods and goddesses into their own traditions when they began to expand throughout Europe and West Asia under the banner of the eagle. Celtic tribes of North West Europe were their fiercest opponents who managed to sack Rome in 387 BCE.

The Celtic Serpent

Snakes for the Celtic cultures were perceived as an embodiment of graceful travel over any terrain and transformative creatures with healing powers and a deep connection with the underworld. The Celtic serpent was also connected to healing pools and springs.

To ensure good fortune in matters of justice, a certain type of egg shaped stone called a 'serpent's egg' was used in a ritual to influence a positive outcome. In the summer, thousands of snakes entwined themselves into a ball, held together by a secretion from their bodies. The hissing serpents spat out their spittle into the air and caught in a cloak before it hit the ground. The druid would then make a hasty escape on horseback when the snakes chased them until a stream cut them off. The serpent egg could be tested for its potency by seeing if it floated against the flow of a river. It was said that these 'eggs' could only be taken on a certain phase of the moon.

Serpents, or more precisely the adder, or nathair in the Celtic tongue has been associated with the Mother Goddess Danu who ruled the rivers and lakes. Danu was the queen of the Tuatha de Danaan, 'People of the goddess Danu', who arrived into Ireland one evening in a cloud. Danu means 'waters of heaven'.

The spring goddess of the forge, Briget is seen as an aspect of Danu, who presides over rivers and lakes and the patron of fertility and poetry. At Imbolc, or the Christian St. Briget's Day on February 1st is when the goddess descends to the earth to spark spring into life with her sacred staff. In some parts of

Scotland, it was also the day of snake worship when pagans gathered to witness a white snake emerge from its underground lair. The white snake would supposedly hold its tail in its mouth as a symbol of rebirth and regeneration.

The Celtic serpent goddess Corra or Corchen was associated with rebirth, healing and wisdom. Corra was of the earth but could transform into a crane and soar into the heavens. St. Patrick has been given the credit for cleansing Ireland of all its snakes, a metaphor for ridding the green isle of its pagan ways. One story has the saint chasing Corra all across Ireland in the 5th Century AD, finally trapping her at Lough Derg or Dragon Lake. Lough Derg was an important sacred site for the druids, with several islands in the lake. Corra was defeated here and all the snakes left Ireland. Druids were known as adders or nathairs by the Celtic tribes, serpent kings, so when St. Patrick banished all the serpents from Ireland it simply meant the final triumph of Christianity over the 'Old Religion', the druids, or druidae (sorcerer) as the Romans called them, and the worship of Corra.

Way of the Serpent

Of all the animal symbols, the snake is the most complex and ancient of them all. Universally, the snake represents the primordial creator force that was in touch with the earth spirits generating the hills and valleys, the water and the cause of all natural phenomenon like earthquakes and floods. It was a symbol of immense power for the early human that affected everything on the planet. The creative and destructive forces attributed to the serpent illustrates its dualistic nature and its recognition as a fertility deity by destroying the old to allow new existences to be born in the physical realm. One of the most well-known symbols portraying snakes is the caduceus, two entwined serpents spiralling around a central rod or wand topped with a bird or pair of wings. The central rod represents universal power, the two snakes wisdom, and the wings represent spiritual awareness. The caduceus signifies the integration of the four main elements; the wand corresponds to the power of the earth, the wings to the attribute of air and the two serpents, the forces of the undulating waves of fire and water.

The symbol of the caduceus can be traced back as far as the Sumerian empire, found in the design of the sacrificial cup of King Gudea of Lagash who reigned between 2144 and 2124 BCE. The Mesopotamians considered the intertwining serpents as a symbol of the god of vegetation and rebirth, Damu, a son of Enki, a known healer and an exorcist, associated with transformation and transition. The Hindu Indians perceived the rod of the caduceus as corresponding to the axis of the world and the serpents as the kundalini force.

The symmetrical arrangement of the two serpents expresses the balancing of opposing forces, an essential law of the universe in creating a higher state of consciousness within the human condition. The balanced duality of the serpents in combination with the wings emphasises a supreme state of self-control in both the physical plane and the higher realm simultaneously. On a deep esoteric level, it is recognised that the serpent of wisdom is directly related to the serpent of evil in the sense that the serpent of wisdom can only slough off its old skin that represents darkness. The two serpents reflect the two opposing polarities of light and darkness, good and evil etc. which lie behind the creative nature of the universe. The Caduceus is the symbol of Hermes and Mercury, the Greek and Roman gods who bought the wisdom of heaven to humanity, which is why they are known as the messenger of the gods.

A single serpent wrapped around a rod is linked to the 'Philosophical Mercury', or the 'Philosophers Stone', is one of the most common esoteric symbols representing secret knowledge. It is also known as the 'Rod of Asclepius', a single serpent entwined rod wielded by the Greek god of healing and medicine, Asclepius. The serpent, with its ability to change its skin symbolises, as we have seen, rebirth and fertility. This symbol has continued to be used in modern times associated with medicine and health care.

A particular type of non-venomous snake was often used in healing rituals and crawled around freely on the floor where the sick and injured slept. From around 300 BCE onwards the cult of Asclepius grew very popular in Greece and pilgrims flocked to his healing temples to be cured of their illnesses. Ritual purification would be followed by offerings or sacrifices and the patient would then spend the night in the holiest part of the sanctuary. Any dreams or visions would be reported to the priest who would then prescribe the appropriate therapy. Products deriving from the venom of snakes were known to make up the majority of medicines.

The daughter of Asclepius and Epione was Hygieia, from where we get the word Hygiene, was a goddess of health and cleanliness. She was associated with the prevention of sickness and the continuation of good health. Hygieia is often depicted collecting the venom into a goblet from a serpent entwined around a large shrub.

A snake on the Tau or T cross represents the death of the lower passions of spiritual growth. The Tau cross, so named because it resembles the Greek capital letter tau denotes the descent of the spirit from a higher plane to the realm of the earth. Traditionally, the standard cross represents the human condition of the created world. It is a combination of the merging of the spiritual with the physical (|) and linear time (—). When the vertical line comes from the horizontal line (T) as in the Tau, it is said to represent the creative ray emerging from the maternal womb, i.e. the human spirit emerging from the mother. With the vertical line indicating the connection between heaven and earth, it is not uncommon for occultists to add a serpent bound to the tau to indicate wisdom gained by someone successfully making the ascent into the spiritual realm. The neophyte initiated into secret wisdom were tied to a T cross and subjected to certain rituals enabling them to develop an inner vision normally hidden from the public. The serpent nailed to the tau cross reflects the darker side of humanity dying so their spirit can find redemption, allowing for their resurrection as an enlightened being.

A crowned snake is recognised as a basilisk, an occult symbol that has the power to destroy anything it gazes upon. It is the magical representation of wisdom, warding off anyone not prepared for its spiritual light who could be blinded by its brilliance. A basilisk swallowing a person symbolises the process of initiation. Initiation is a Latin term meaning 'entering into the spiritual realm', or into wisdom by entering into the serpent's (or fish's) body. It symbolises a person who has been granted vision into both the physical and spiritual worlds.

The many images of snake (and fish) tailed humans are magical impressions portraying initiation towards wisdom. They symbolise where the neophyte has so integrated themselves in the way of wisdom that they have become the serpent itself.

A coiled basilisk is associated with the family of Dan, one of the twelve tribes of Israel who were associated with the astrological sign of Scorpio. In magical terms, Scorpio can also be represented by the eagle, denoting the nature of the scorpion has been redeemed and is able to ascend to heaven. Some imagery illustrates a dead snake in the mouth or talons of the redeemed eagle symbolising the lower nature of the serpent has been defeated and higher planes of existence is open for ascension.

Traditionally, the coiled serpent suggests a pent up energy ready to be released like a wound up spring. The spiral of the snake expresses nature and in the form of the basilisk suggests danger and will confront the unprepared with its viscous bite. Pent up energies, danger, initiation and wisdom are all qualities associated with Scorpio. My fiancée and my best friend are both Scorpio's, should I be worried? The spiral is a magical journey from the tip of the tail on the outside towards the centre where illumination can be found at the head of the serpent.

Another popular symbol of a snake is of one eating its own tail known as an ouroboros. It represents at a basic level the cycles of time from which wisdom springs and is the highest spiritual energy of the gods. The symbol signifies the continued cycle of day and night and the changing seasons. It reflects the life, death and rebirth nature of the universe. The circle of the ouroboros contains the whole cosmos and symbolises eternity.

The shape of the letter S is perceived as representing the snake in some cultures. It is seen as an actual form of the path towards wisdom, the undulating way by which wisdom is attained. It represents initiation, the weaving between choices and polarities. In occult terms, the path towards wisdom is referred to as the 'Way of the Serpent.

In the western world since the rise of Greece as a superpower, the serpent has largely been a symbol of an enemy or Satan, the chaos within the order of democracy. With its forked tongue suggesting hypocrisy and deceit and its venom capable of bringing a sudden and painful death, the serpent has become a representative of negativity and something to fear, something the Christian church were happy to take advantage of.

Chinese Serpents

The Chinese universe came into existence when elements swimming in a vast cloud of moisture were ordered into the opposing forces of Yin and Yang. With the interaction of the opposites, everything in the universe was created. Yin was perceived as the spirit of the tiger and Yang the force of the dragon. Before heaven and earth existed, there was chaos that contained all the elements for creation to exist. It took the form of a moist darkness within a giant egg. At its heart, Pan Gu slept for 18,000 years, slowly growing in the mist of formlessness until he woke in the form of a short muscular man holding a chisel in one hand and an axe in the other. Pan Gu used the tools to break out of the egg, sending the elements of creation flying through space. The lighter, purer parts (Yang) rose upwards to form the heaven and the heavier impure particles (Yin) sank to form the earth.

Pan Gu found himself stood on the earth with the sky resting on his head trying to fall back into the earth's embrace forcing Pan Gu to keep pushing them apart to keep them separated. After another 18,000 years, when Pan Gu was fully stretched with the earth at his toes and the heaven at his fingertips, the point was reached where the sky and the ground were far enough distance apart to resist each other's attraction. Pan Gu's breath became the winds, his voice was the thunder, his left eye the sun and his right eye the moon. His hair and beard became the stars and his sweat the rain. His hands and feet became the four corners of the earth and his body transformed into five sacred mountains. His blood became the rivers and lakes, his flesh the fertile fields, his teeth and bones were the minerals and rocks and his semen became precious pearls and jade.

The five sacred mountains became the four points of the compass with the fifth sitting at the centre. The eastern mountain was associated with the green dragon, the season of spring and the element wood. The southern mountain was home to the red phoenix, summer and fire. The west mountain belonged to the white tiger, autumn and metal and the north mountain was the black tortoise-snake hybrid, known as the black warrior, winter and water. The fifth mountain was China itself, associated with the colour yellow and the element earth.

The first of three rulers of China was the Lord of Heaven who took the form of a great serpent with the feet of a wild animal. He had twelve heads and ruled for 18,000 years. His successor, the Lord of the Earth had an identical appearance and reigned for the same amount of time. The third ruler was the Lord of Man who presided over the first of the 'Ten Epochs', teaching the people of China to plough the land and grow crops.

The Chinese mother goddess was Nü Wa, a human headed serpent who created the first human beings. After the earth and heaven came into being, Nü Wa roamed the land admiring the waters full of fish and the countryside teeming with wild animals. She thought the world was a wonderful place to live but could not ignore the fact she felt lonely with no one to talk and play with. Looking at her reflection in a pond Nü Wa decided how good it would be if she had some companions to have fun with and took it upon herself to make her own friends. She took a handful of mud from the water's edge and moulded it into a body with two arms, two legs and a head. As soon as she put it on the ground, it came to life and scrambled around on the grass. Nü Wa was so pleased with the being she set about making more humans before the sun in his chariot, drawn by dragons had finished his journey across the heavens. The following morning Nü Wa continued to make people but it was very time consuming and wanting to fill the whole world with humans came up with a plan. She took a reed from the riverbank, dipped it in the mud and swung it around so the drops of mud flew off onto the ground. As the clods of mud landed, they turned into people and in no time at all, Nü Wa soon populated all of the earth. In some versions of the myth, the people Nü Wa created by hand were the emperors and kings and those she flicked from the reed were the peasants.

For many years humanity lived a happy life until a quarrel began between Gong Gong, the spirit of water who had a human head of copper, an iron forehead, red hair and a body of a serpent, and his father Zhurong, the spirit of fire, an armour clad human warrior with a sword, riding a tiger. Their bickering caused the northern sky to tilt towards the ground and great cracks to open up in the earth where waters flooded out covering the plains. On higher ground, fire ravaged the forests forcing the whole of the northwest to rise up, draining the rivers and lakes to the southwest where they gathered to form the seas we see there today. Wild beasts stampeded in fear, running down and killing people who got in their way and birds desperate for food swooped down to peck the flesh from the bones of the dead. The seasons fell out of their normal order causing nature to wither and begin to die. Nü Wa had to act quickly to repair the damage, taking some rocks from a swollen river and built a massive fire, melting them into a thick paste, which she used to patch up the sky. Then she cut off the legs of a tortoise and used them as pillars to support the heaven at the four corners of the world to stop it collapsing again. When she was happy with the repair, Nü Wa calmed down the frightened animals and controlled the floodwaters by building dykes made from the ashes of burned reeds. Order quickly returned and peace between humans and animals was re-established and crops grew again in fertile land. The balance of heaven and earth was restored once more.

The husband and brother of Nü Wa was the serpent king Fu Hsi (great brilliance) who was believed to be the father of our present civilisation. In the beginning, there was no social order amongst the people created by Nü Wa. Children only knew their mothers and when hungry, people searched for food and clothed themselves in skins and rushes. When Fu Hsi arrived, he looked upwards to the heavens, then down to the occurrences on earth, and saw the potential of the human race. First, he united man with a wife and laid down the laws of humanity by devising the eight trigrams and the 64 hexagrams of the I Ching and its application so that humans could gain mastery over the world. Fu Hsi taught humanity the use of fire, how to build homes and live in communities and introduced stringed instruments for playing music. He taught how to knot cord for fishing nets and baskets and how to attach a handle to a split piece of wood to make ploughs.

Depictions of Nü Wa and Fu Hsi as human headed serpents entwined around each other indicating their Yin and Yang partnership are found all across China. Some images portray them with wings symbolising their immortality and their connection with heaven.

The ninth emperor Yu the Great ruled China around 2,200 BCE succeeding the popular Shun who had divided the empire into twelve provinces. Eight years into his reign, word reached Yu of a monstrous giant serpent with nine heads called Xiangliu was terrorising an outlying district of his realm. The serpent was an old ambassador of Yu's old flood era enemy Gong Gong, sent to cause havoc in the newly ordered lands. Each of the nine heads spat out a venom so toxic that it annihilated vast amounts of countryside where it landed. Xiangliu was so large it could wrap itself around nine separate hills. Yu hoped to take the serpent by surprised when it rested, but even when it slept, its heads were constantly scanning all directions making an unseen attack impossible. Yu noticed that the serpent never looked up, obviously not expecting danger from the air which gave Yu an idea. Climbing aboard his trusty old dragon and armed with a sword, Yu soared up into the sky until he was directly above Xiangliu and swooped down, cutting off two heads before the serpent was aware it was under attack. A ferocious battle began between man and serpent with Xiangliu's remaining heads thrashing this way and that, making it difficult for Yu to make any contact at all. However, Yu persisted and after lopping off the final head, the serpent convulsed as it hit the ground, dead. From the mouths of the fallen heads, venom spewed out destroying great tracts of land with poison seeping into the ground water polluting the local rivers and lakes. Yu finally solved the problem by burying the heads on an island in an artificial lake whose waters soaked up the remaining toxins and insulated the neighbouring districts from contamination.

There be Dragons

You cannot write about China without mentioning dragons. Traditionally, dragons are serpents with wings and talons, a combination of a snake and an eagle or some other bird of prey. It symbolises the ascension of the spirit from the gross earth to the lighter spirit of heaven, the realm of the gods and goddesses, angels and jinn. The Chinese regarded dragons as an entirely separate species from the serpent and a powerful force in their own right. Like the serpent, dragons have their origins as rain and water deities, living in rivers and lakes. The most powerful dragons ruled the seas, rivers and lakes. They would ascend to heaven once a year to report to their overlord, the Jade Emperor, the activities on earth so the celestial king could manage its affairs. They were invoked in times of drought with the Dragon Dance, still being performed at Chinese New Year festivals today. Some believe they were connected with the Yellow Springs underground stream, which the sun travelled during the night.

Chinese dragons were generally considered protectors and guardians, keeping watch over the water and the sky. Their benevolent nature and great power gave reason for China's emperors to appropriate the dragon as an imperial symbol. They were held to be the ancestors of the rulers of ancient times.

An emperor from the Xia dynasty collected the saliva from the mouths of two ancient kings who appeared to him as dragons, locked it away in a chest and stored it in his palace. Centuries later, the tenth ruler of the Zhou dynasty discovered it and when he opened the chest, the saliva spread throughout the palace. Aware of its potential, the emperor ordered all of his wives to strip naked and several of them became pregnant from the dragon spit, creating a direct link between the existing ruling family and the dragon kings of China's remote past.

A popular fairy tale speaks of when a student from Suzhou City called Liu Yi came across a young woman crying by the roadside, he stops to console her and dry her tears. The woman reveals to the student that she was the youngest daughter of the dragon king of Dongting Lake and was sad because she had been spurned by her husband, the son of a river god and made to take human form. Learning that Liu Yi was heading to the lake, the woman quickly wrote a letter and asks the student to pass it on to her father to inform him of her plight. In his crystal palace at the bottom of the lake, the dragon king read the letter with deep concern. He quickly dispatched a dragon to rescue his daughter and return her home to the lakebed. As it happened, the woman's husband dies suddenly and in gratitude for bringing the news to his attention, the dragon king offers Liu Yi his daughters hand in marriage. The woman returns to the human world to live with Liu Yi as man and wife to live happily ever after.

Feathered Serpent

There was a dark void in the beginning of the Mayan world containing nothing but the sky and the sea where several gods lived. When a god from each of the realms began speaking with each other, the world came into being. The sky god was Hurricane who manifested as a bolt of lightning and the water god, the Sovereign Plumed Serpent known as Gucumatz or Kukulcan. According to the codex Popol Vuh, the two gods were 'great knowers and thinkers' who instigated life on Earth by the sound of their voices.

Their first task was to shape the Earth by lowering the vast dark waters to expose land allowing trees and vegetation to grow. Then they created wild animals to live in the forests, creatures like jaguars, serpents, deer and birds. Hurricane and Gucumatz desired to be acknowledged and worshipped for bringing the world into existence but none of the animals they created had the ability to pay them homage. Undeterred, the gods went about creating a species that could. Their first attempt were people made out of mud; however, they would simply crumble and fall apart and when it rained would melt back into the Earth. Next, they tried making people out of plants, males from the coral tree and females from the fibrous cores of bulrushes. Unfortunately, for the gods, the people made from plants had no minds or hearts and were vacant of any understanding of thought or feeling and unable to have any devotion to their creators. Disappointed, Hurricane called up a mighty flood and washed them away.

The gods could only be properly honoured when an intelligent human race emerged, so for a third attempt, Hurricane and Gucumatz called on the help of the fox, the coyote, the parrot and the crow to get it right this time round. The animals searched the land for a suitable ingredient to make humans from before discovering maize from a mountainous area called 'Bitter Water

Place'. They gathered bundles of the plant and took it to the goddess Xmucane who mixed the grain with water to make a dough before passing it on to Hurricane and Gucumatz. From the maize dough, four men with awareness and intelligence were created who regularly showed their appreciation to the gods that made them. The sky and water gods were finally pleased with their work.

The men had a thirst for knowledge and understanding and began to spend most of their time investigating the world they lived in and spent less and less time honouring their creators. When their comprehension of the universe began to rival that of the gods, Hurricane and Gucumatz decided something needed to be done. To distract the men from their search of knowledge, four women were created who gave birth to many tribes that quickly spread across the land ensuring the men were kept busy keeping them all under control. The descendants of the maize people were very obedient and honoured the gods on a regular basis. When they prayed for light, the gods promised them a sun and told them to look towards the east for the arrival of a star that would be heralded in by the planet Venus.

Up until now, the Mayans had wandered in the darkness using fire for their light and warmth. In the darkness, there was no conception of any social order leaving the people of Middle America to wander aimlessly in search for their place in the world. However, the first dawn was so long in coming, the wanderers became disheartened and looked for new gods to venerate. Hurricane became angry at the Mayans change of allegiance so punished them with a heavy hailstorm that extinguished all their fires leaving the Earth sodden and his people cold and blind. Seeing the humans shivering in the dark, the fire god Tohil offered them his flames in return for blood sacrifices. This involved the removal of a victims still beating heart from a hole made in the rib cage. Desperate for light and warmth, the Mayans agreed.

Whether this had any bearing on the eventual arrival of the sun is anyone's guess, but suddenly, without warning, the first dawn began, heralded in as promised by the planet Venus. As the sun rose, the Earth quickly dried out, the birds spread their wings and began to sing and the humans knelt to the ground and prayed to the heavenly light. At first, the sun's power was so intense that it turned the old gods and all the wild animals into stone, but as time passed, the sun's energy abated making life on Earth more comfortable for all living things.

The 'Fifth Sun', is the age of the present time according to the Aztecs who performed constant rituals to ensure the universal balance between heaven and Earth was always maintained. Four Suns, or ages have already been and gone, each one associated with an element and a compass point. Different races have lived in each era and were destroyed or transformed when their age was terminated by a new god. The 'First Sun', was associated with the Earth and populated by mindless vegetarian giants. This first world was ruled by the brothers Tezcatlipoca, the sun god known as the dark destroyer, and the water god, Quetzalcoatl, the 'Plumed or Feathered Serpent', an old god the Aztecs imported from older Mexican civilizations. Quetzalcoatl was associated with water, both of the Earth and in the sky as rain. He represented both fertility and life itself. His power was seen as regenerative and life giving because he linked the Earth with the heavens. The serpent god has been depicted rearing from the Earth Mother to Tlaloc, the god of rain and lightning. As the wind god Ehecatl, Quetzalcoatl was credited for the winds that bought rain clouds that watered the parched lands. The serpent god was also often identified with one of the earliest Mexican deities, Kukulcan, a dragon of the sky who was seen as the beloved agricultural god of spring and vegetation. Kukulcan would punish humanity with tornados and waterspouts when he was angry with them. The Plumed Serpent was also identified with the Aztec priesthood with the most important holy men having the title Quetzalcoatl. In this incarnation, Quetzalcoatl was depicted as a fair-skinned man with long white hair and beard dressed in black robes wearing a pointed conical hat looking much like how we imagine a wizard or witch today. As his manifestation as the priest-king Topiltzin, Quetzalcoatl sacrificed himself at the end of his reign by cremating himself on a pyre. As flames consumed his body, his heart ascended into the heavens to become the 'Morning Star', of Venus, the 'Light Bringer'. From Venus, Quetzalcoatl promised to return to Earth one day to establish a new kingdom of peace and harmony.

Whether it was divine intervention or astonishing good luck, when the conquistadors arrived in Mexico in 1519 they were first spotted on the very day Quetzalcoatl was prophesised to return. The king of the Aztecs, Montezuma believed them to be the returning Feathered Serpent coming to establish a new world order on Earth and welcomed them with open arms. With the conquistadors dressed in metal armour and their priests dressed in black robes similar to their own priests and with their message of brotherly love, it is easy to see why the Aztecs were convinced it was the returning Quetzalcoatl. The Spanish story of a sacrificed Christ who was resurrected echoed the story of Topiltzin almost exactly, convincing Montezuma to offer them gold and peace. In return the Spanish gave slaughter and a devastating plague we know as the common cold that swept through Mesoamerica killing most of the Aztec people.

Quetzalcoatl of the 'First Sun', was jealous of his brother Tezcatlipoca shining bright in the sky so beat him with his staff, forcing the first age sun god to flee into the waters surrounding the Earth where Tezcatlipoca transformed into a jaguar and ate the entire race of giants. The second age, the Sun of Wind, was created and ruled by Quetzalcoatl in the form of the wind god Ehecatl. The people of this age lived as simple vegetarians with slightly more intelligence than the giants. All the people were swept away by a great hurricane, blowing them into the jungle where the survivors transformed into monkeys. The third world, the 'Sun of Rain', was governed by Tlaloc, the god of rain and fertility. This age saw humanity discover agriculture and farming. This world ended when Quetzalcoatl sent a rain of fiery ash, transforming the survivors into butterflies, dogs and turkeys.

Chalchiuhtlicue, 'She of the Jade Skirt', was the creator of the fourth world, the 'Sun of Water'. She was the wife of Tlaloc and the goddess of rivers, lakes and oceans. This world was destroyed when the goddess caused the waters below the Earth to rise to the surface causing a great flood. The people of the fourth age transformed into fish. At the same time, the sky collapsed causing chaos and darkness to reign for a time. The fearsome goddess Tlaltecuhtli would only allow crops to grow if she was fed with human blood. The brothers Tezcatlipoca and Quetzalcoatl putting their differences aside for a moment transformed into giant serpents and tore the bloodthirsty goddess in two. They cast her top half into the sky to become the vault of heaven and her bottom half to form the Earth. To restore humans onto the Earth, Quetzalcoatl travelled to the underworld to search for what was left of the fish people and took their remains to the Aztec paradise 'Land of the Misty Sky'. With his fellow gods, the 'Plumed Serpent' ground the bones of the fish people, mixed it with their own blood into a dough and fashioned it into people. Then they nurtured them until they were ready to be sent to earth as a fully evolved culture at the start of the Fifth and present Sun.

Aztec prophecy reveals that the end of the 'Fifth Sun' will be destroyed by earthquakes. It will come when the world is consumed by conflict and famine, when unscrupulous leaders rule nations and their people divided over almost everything. After the earthquakes, time will come to an end forever. The end of the world is inescapable but it can be postponed indefinitely by satisfying the gods through ritual and human sacrifice, which could explain why wars have ravaged across the planet for the past 1,000 years or more.

Snake Bites

Snake superstition, folk lore and other serpent oddities

- The American Hopi Indians associated the snake with Mother Earth. They saw them as the umbilical cord that connects humanity to nature.
- The Cherokee associated the snake with great cosmic power. They believed that if a person dreamt a snake bit them, they should be treated as if they had received a real snake bite because the snake in the dream was a ghost snake.
- The powdered rattles of a rattlesnake made into a drink would assist a mother during a difficult birth.
- Kentuckians believed that the rattles worn as hair decoration prevented headaches.
- In Punjab, India, it is believed that anyone bitten by a snake could be cured by smoking the feathers of a peacock.

- In England, if a pregnant woman is frightened by a snake, it is said her child would be born with a constricted throat.
- If a live adder is found on a doorstep, death in the household is imminent.
- Adder skin worn around the affected part could cure rheumatism.
- The dried skin of a snake hung over a fireplace in some parts of Britain would protect the house from fire and bring good fortune to the family.
- In 1909, American George Went Hensley perceived the scriptures commanded the faithful to handle serpents. He introduced the practice to churches in Tennessee and Kentucky and spread into neighbouring states. Hensley got his inspiration from John 3:14-15 when Jesus revealed to the Rabbi Nicodemus that only those born of spirit can enter the kingdom of god. *As Moses lifted up the bronze snake on a pole in the desert in the same way the 'Son of Man' must be lifted up, so that everyone who believes in Him may have eternal life'.* This story refers to the exodus of the Israelites nearing the promised land of fertile Canaan after nearly forty years wandering in the desert. The tribe of nomads began to complain to Moses about their ordeal lasting so long. YHWH heard their concerns and sent down poisonous snakes among them and many were bitten and died. Moses prayed to the Lord to remove the snakes away from his people. YHWH told Moses to construct a bronze serpent and put it on a pole for anyone who was bitten could look at it and be healed. Numbers 21:4-9. The snakes used in Henley's church services were gathered beforehand. Rattlesnakes, water moccasins and copperheads were kept in a box throughout the service, then taken out and handed around the congregation. In some churches, the snakes were released onto the

floor for the believers to wrap them over their head and around their body and even kiss them as proof of their faith in God.

- Early August 1705, the village of Markopoulos on the Greek island of Kefalonia was attacked and ransacked by pirates. Not wishing to be raped and sold into slavery, the nuns of a monastery dedicated to 'Our Lady of Langouvarda', prayed fervently to the 'Virgin', for protection. The nuns were miraculously transformed into European Cat snakes (Telescopus fallax) who are hostile and aggressive creatures ensuring the pirates left them alone. Since then, the snakes have returned each year to the site between the 5th and 15th of August. To commemorate the occasion the 'Miracle of the Snakes of Theotokos (Mother Mary) is celebrated on the 'Feast of the Dormition', when the small black snakes appear at the church of Panagia of Langouvarde that now sits on the site of the old monastery. The snakes have a small cross on the head and their tongues are in the shape of the cross. They appear in and around the courtyard of the church, on the walls and on the bell tower. The snakes show no fear while the services are held and are harmless during the festivities. As soon as the celebrations are over on the 15th of August, they return to being aggressive and disappear back into the wilderness until the same time the following year. The islanders consider them to be holy and place them on a silver icon of the 'Virgin of the Snakes'. The snakes have only failed to appear on two occasions, once during the Second World War and again in 1953 before a destructive earthquake hit the island later that year. The villagers believe that if the snakes fail to appear anytime between the 5th and 15th of August, something catastrophic is coming to the island.

- American Bill Haast injected himself with snake venom

for several years to build up an immunity against the poison. He survived 172 bites and donated his blood to cure snake bite victims. Haast was the owner and operator of the Miami Serpentarium tourist attraction south of Miami, Florida from 1947 to 1984. He died of natural causes aged 100 in June 2011.

- Known locally as the snake man, Filipino Bernardo Alverez claimed to be immune to snake venom, died aged 62 in July 2021 when a cobra bit him on the tongue when he tried to kiss it. Angry locals killed the snake afterwards.

- Cleopatra was born in 69 BCE and ruled Egypt from 51 to 30 BCE. She formed an alliance with Rome by taking, first Julius Caesar, then Mark Antony as lovers. When Gaius Octavian aka Augustus succeeded his great uncle Julius Caesar, Mark Antony and Cleopatra opposed his rule and a war broke out between the two sides. When Octavian defeated Antony and Cleopatra's naval fleet in 31 BCE, he invaded Egypt and made it a province of the Roman Empire. Antony and Cleopatra made a pact to take their lives rather than submit to Octavian's rule. On the 1st of August, Mark Antony committed suicide by stabbing himself through the stomach. Before Cleopatra could kill herself, she was rounded up and put under house arrest in her palace. Octavian wished to parade the great Egyptian queen in chains around Rome. Not wanting the intimidation, an asp, believed to be a cobra, a symbol of Egyptian divine royalty was smuggled past her guards in a basket of figs. On August 12th, Cleopatra, either from the serpent's bite or the poison administered herself using a hatpin committed suicide aged 39 to join her lover Mark Antony in the realm of the dead.

- The Naga's were serpent like water deities, generally depicted as human heads on the body of a snake.

Sometimes they are shown as a face in the expanded neck of a cobra and other times as a human from the waist up with a serpents tail below like the Greek goddess Echidna, the 'Mother of all Monsters'. Naga's were also portrayed as many headed serpents like Ananta on whose belly Vishnu slept while dreaming up the next creation. They were the children of the rishi Kashapa and Kudra. Naga's were semi divine deities associated with rivers, lakes, wells and the sea who were exiled to the underworld by Brahman when they became too popular with the Hindu people. They have been described as powerful and proud and took a beneficial protagonist role in Hindu mythology.

- One of the most iconic goddess figures is the Minoan snake goddess, the one with her breasts exposed from her checked skirt, her arms outstretched holding a serpent in each hand and a cat sat on her hat. When she was excavated, she lacked a head and half her left arm. In her right hand, she held what was described as a striped wavy stick at the time when the British archaeologist Sir Arthur Evans excavated the Palace of Minos at Knossos on the island of Crete between 1899 and 1903. Using a complete goddess figurine discovered in the Temple Repositories, which had snakes slithering up both arms as an example, Evans, with Danish artist Halvor Bagge restored the incomplete goddess with a matching left arm complete with a stripy serpent. They added a head with a hat and a cat from the items they unearthed from the Temple Repositories.

- Serpent Mound is an ancient archaeological site in Peebles, Ohio, USA. It is the largest earthwork of a serpent in the world at 1,348 feet long and 3 feet high, estimated to have been constructed around 300 BCE. It is on the site of an ancient meteor impact from around 300 million years ago. The construction is unique and represents a major accomplishment for the early native culture. The mound consists of a thick layer of ash and clay, held in place by a layer of rocks. On top of that is a thick layer of soil allowing grass and other vegetation to cover the mound. It is possible it had a spiritual purpose given that many native cultures in North and Central America revered snakes and attributed supernatural powers to them. The design of the mound reflects the shape of the constellation Draco. It winds back and forth for more than 800 feet with seven distinct curves and ends in a triple coiled tail. In the open jaws of the serpent is believed to be the egg of life being swallowed (or regurgitated). Researchers Clark and Marjorie Hardman discovered the head of the serpent and egg align to the setting summer solstice sun. They also noticed that the curves in the body relates to the sunrise at both solstices and the equinoxes.

- The 'Temple of Kukulcan or 'Feathered Serpent', dominates the centre of one of the largest Mayan cities, Chichen Itza that thrived between 600 and 1200 AD. The 98-foot high pyramid including the temple on top is built of limestone and designated by archaeologists as Structure 5B18. Its four stairways has 91 steps each and with the top platform counting as a step, totals 365, the number of days in a solar year. During the spring and autumn equinoxes, the pyramid serves as a visual symbol of the balance of day and night. The late afternoon sun creates the illusion of a snake creeping slowly down the northern staircase. Light and shadow combine to show an undulating giant serpent descending to the Earth. This spectacle creates seven triangles on the side of the staircase connecting the top platform with the giant stone feathered serpent head at the bottom representing Kukulcan's return to the Earth to provide blessings for a full harvest and good health to his worshippers, lasting for around 45 minutes. Symbolically, the 'Feathered Serpent connects the three worlds of heaven, Earth and the underworld with the balance and harmony of the opposing forces of light and dark.

Epilogue

When the serpent speaks, it is important that you listen, for it is the wisdom of the universe. The serpent is your intuition, your gut feeling, your inner instinct. The spirit of the serpent is very ancient and within us all. The serpent is the power of creation that allows us to exist and with its duality of opposing forces, transforms energy so we are born, live and die allowing nature to grow and evolve. The Stone Age Mother Goddess knew this and with the knowledge of the serpent, educated humanity to think for itself, to become individuals and separate from the wild animals they shared the Earth with.

Humanity learnt to control fire, make stone tools and understood the importance of the cycles and phases of the moon and sun. They made stone circles, pillars and rows as timepieces so they knew the best time to hunt and gather to ensure their survival. Then something changed, a new oppressive power took over subjugating humanity to domestication and easily controllable. They were put to work constructing temples, cities and industries under the order of priest-kings who served their gods and goddesses created from natural forces like the power of the wind and water and the influences of the planets, sun and moon. The connection with the Earth spirit was broken and humanity fell into a deep enchantment void of true spirituality and compassion. Until we remember and recognise the spirit in all things and within ourselves, we will always struggle to interact with the spirit of nature, the essence of Mother Earth. Humanity as a whole has forgotten that we are all spiritual beings in physical bodies.

As we have learnt from the creation myths mentioned in this book, civilisations have come and gone because the gods have not been happy with the way they have turned out. We have gone through several ages of humankind before our present one. Throughout all of the different creations, the serpent has survived them all. The snake has been around for many millions of years, slithering among the dinosaurs, the mud and plant people, the fish people and still around to influence Adam and Eve, the first Homo sapiens. Today, the serpent is thriving on all the habitable continents and will still be around long after we as a species have been replaced by a better version of a human being. According to the creation myths, each age had a god or goddess that designed and created it and all have a serpent somewhere in the story, all promising to return someday to see out the old era that will be destroyed and prepare for a new 'kingdom of god', for the next stage of humanity.

Without doubt, the serpent represents a divine energy that gives life and growth to our planet before destroying it for something new.

The serpent, as we have seen, is both fire and water, opposing forces in one body, much like the Babylonian powers of Ishtar and Ereshkigal, fertility goddesses of life and death who are also associated with Earth's sister planet Venus, the 'Light bringer', or Lucifer. Most people understand this energy better as Yin and Yang, the dark and light forces that create and drive our existence. It is the dynamic of the opposing forces that created everything and in most of the ancient cultures; the serpent was one and sometimes both of those opposing powers.

The first recorded goddess, the Mother of Life, the Sumerian/ Babylonian Tiamat was described as an infinite mass of 'water' that contained all the ingredients of life. When she merged with the opposing force of Apsu, an infinite mass of pure 'water', a third force was created, the vitality of 'chaos', from which order arose in the form of natural phenomenon like air and water, fire and matter from which the gods took their names. These powers/ gods interacted to give birth to more elements and gods. When the new gods became powerful, they destroyed the 'Mother' that gave them life, portraying her as an evil serpent, a 'She Dragon' who stood in their way of a new kingdom on Earth.

The demonising of the Mother Goddess/serpent was the demonising of all women and the suppression of the feminine (Yin) energy in most men. The male had to be macho, controlling and strong or else he would not survive. We all have Shakti, the kundalini within each of us. Sometimes she is the sweet Parvati or the quiet Durga. Sometimes she is the wild Kali who takes no nonsense from anyone. It is through Shakti energy we reach the cosmic forces of heaven (Shiva), the god energy. Of course, those in power that run governments and religions do not want this. With the knowledge of the universe, the wisdom of the serpent, our leaders would no longer have any power over us.

The serpent is a survivor because it can adapt to any condition the universe throws at it. We know this because it has been around for 167 million years and one of the few creatures to do so. There have been many Ice Ages and glacial expansions during their existence and despite being cold-blooded reptiles that need the warmth to live have done very well. Like all reptiles and many mammals, serpents need to hibernate during cold spells. With glacial expansions lasting many centuries, the serpent would have gone deep underground (into the underworld) living in darkness relying on smell, sound and touch to find prey. In the same way, to be human is to delve into our own darkness within to deal with our baggage that keeps us bound to the physical realm.

Earth spirits are powerful energies that humanity has lost its connection with over the last few millennia. The same could be said concerning the animal spirits we once worked with. Whatever animal you feel attached to, it is important that you spend time meditating on it. By connecting with your animal spirit, you are at the same time connecting to the Earth spirits and the 'Mother' herself. It is snakes that are the guardians to the portals between worlds, a window into the supernatural. The serpent has the power of wisdom, the force of transformation and the energy behind life and death and of creation and destruction. It is both a masculine and feminine force in one body, as are we when we recognise that fact and allow them to permeate into our everyday life. We often hear of something needing a woman's touch but there is no reason at all a man cannot be capable of nurturing, caring and being emotional or a woman being a leader, confident and emotionally strong.

A little bit of cunning can be useful at times, cunning beats strength every time. Just look at Ulysses and the Cyclops, Perseus and Medusa and Isis and Ra who used cunning to get what they wanted, and of course, the cunning of the Greeks with the Trojan horse, about as cunning as cunning can be. When you feel threatened by anything or anyone, call on the serpent energy to protect you, focus on the kundalini of Shakti to see you through. Hiss, spit, and give the evil stare if you have to. Walk away if possible but if you get backed into a corner, rattle your tail and fight for all you are worth. When things get ugly, saddle up and ride the serpent into battle.

Selected Bibliography

Collins, Andrew – The Cygnus Mystery, 2006

Cotterell, Arthur – World Mythology, 1979

Cotterell, Arthur & Storm, Rachel – The Ultimate Encyclopaedia of Mythology, 1999

Douglas, Nik & Slinger, Penny – Sexual Secrets, 1979

Goodman, Frederick – Magic Symbols, 1989

Hancock, Graham – Fingerprints of the Gods, 1995

Hope, Murray – Practical Greek Magic, 1985

Littleton, C. Scott general editor – Mythology, the Illustrated Anthology of World – Myth and Story Telling, 2002

Mackenzie, Donald – Indian Myths and Legends, 2008

Regardie, Israel – The Golden Dawn, 971

Sams, Jamie & Carson, David – Medicine Cards, 1988

Spence, Lewis – Mysteries of Celtic Britain, 1998

The I Ching or Book of Changes (translated by Brynes, Gary, F., 1950

Wa-Na-Nee-Che with Harvey, Eliana – White Eagle Medicine Wheel, 1997

**MOON
BOOKS**

PAGANISM & SHAMANISM

What is Paganism? A religion, a spirituality, an alternative
belief system, nature worship? You can find support for all these
definitions (and many more) in dictionaries, encyclopaedias, and
text books of religion, but subscribe to any one and the truth will
evade you. Above all Paganism is a creative pursuit, an encounter
with reality, an exploration of meaning and an expression of the
soul. Druids, Heathens, Wiccans and others, all contribute their
insights and literary riches to the Pagan tradition. Moon Books
invites you to begin or to deepen your own encounter, right here,
right now.
If you have enjoyed this book, why not tell other readers by
posting a review on your preferred book site.

Recent bestsellers from Moon Books are:

Journey to the Dark Goddess
How to Return to Your Soul
Jane Meredith
Discover the powerful secrets of the Dark Goddess and
transform your depression, grief and pain into healing
and integration.
Paperback: 978-1-84694-677-6 ebook: 978-1-78099-223-5

Shamanic Reiki
Expanded Ways of Working with Universal Life Force Energy
Llyn Roberts, Robert Levy
Shamanism and Reiki are each powerful ways of healing; together,
their power multiplies. *Shamanic Reiki* introduces techniques to
help healers and Reiki practitioners tap ancient healing wisdom.
Paperback: 978-1-84694-037-8 ebook: 978-1-84694-650-9

Pagan Portals – The Awen Alone
Walking the Path of the Solitary Druid
Joanna van der Hoeven
An introductory guide for the solitary Druid, *The Awen Alone* will
accompany you as you explore, and seek out your own place
within the natural world.
Paperback: 978-1-78279-547-6 ebook: 978-1-78279-546-9

A Kitchen Witch's World of Magical Herbs & Plants
Rachel Patterson
A journey into the magical world of herbs and plants, filled with
magical uses, folklore, history and practical magic. By popular
writer, blogger and kitchen witch, Tansy Firedragon.
Paperback: 978-1-78279-621-3 ebook: 978-1-78279-620-6

Medicine for the Soul
The Complete Book of Shamanic Healing
Ross Heaven
All you will ever need to know about shamanic healing and how to
become your own shaman...
Paperback: 978-1-78099-419-2 ebook: 978-1-78099-420-8

Shaman Pathways – The Druid Shaman
Exploring the Celtic Otherworld
Danu Forest
A practical guide to Celtic shamanism with exercises and
techniques as well as traditional lore for exploring the Celtic
Otherworld.
Paperback: 978-1-78099-615-8 ebook: 978-1-78099-616-5

Traditional Witchcraft for the Woods and Forests
A Witch's Guide to the Woodland with Guided Meditations and
Pathworking
Mélusine Draco
A Witch's guide to walking alone in the woods, with guided
meditations and pathworking.
Paperback: 978-1-84694-803-9 ebook: 978-1-84694-804-6

Wild Earth, Wild Soul
A Manual for an Ecstatic Culture
Bill Pfeiffer
Imagine a nature-based culture so alive and so connected,
spreading like wildfire. This book is the first flame...
Paperback: 978-1-78099-187-0 ebook: 978-1-78099-188-7

Naming the Goddess
Trevor Greenfield
Naming the Goddess is written by over eighty adherents and scholars of Goddess and Goddess Spirituality.
Paperback: 978-1-78279-476-9 ebook: 978-1-78279-475-2

Shapeshifting into Higher Consciousness
Heal and Transform Yourself and Our World with Ancient Shamanic and Modern Methods
Llyn Roberts
Ancient and modern methods that you can use every day to transform yourself and make a positive difference in the world.
Paperback: 978-1-84694-843-5 ebook: 978-1-84694-844-2

Readers of ebooks can buy or view any of these bestsellers by clicking on the live link in the title. Most titles are published in paperback and as an ebook. Paperbacks are available in traditional bookshops. Both print and ebook formats are available online.

Find more titles and sign up to our readers' newsletter at
http://www.johnhuntpublishing.com/paganism
Follow us on Facebook at https://www.facebook.com/MoonBooks
and Twitter at https://twitter.com/MoonBooksJHP